Petals from the Basket
Devotional Thoughts for Women

Brenda Strohbehn

To Dr. Ben and Lorraine Strohbehn

My parents
My mentors
My examples

CONTENTS

ACKNOWLEDGMENT

You, the readers of my blog posts on Petalsfromthe Basket.com, are among the most encouraging and generous people I know. Without you, my basket of words and experiences would be incomplete.

You add the beauty of your lives to the bouquet of mine, and together, we're learning and growing in faith and in grace.

Thank you for being all kinds of wonderful!

INTRODUCTION

The baskets of our lives are filled with petals from work, family, special events, hobbies, and much more! I believe that each petal—even the wilted ones—can represent blessings that God gives us through each season of life. My desire is that as I open my heart and transparently share ideas and resources for everyday Christian living, I will be able to point to the fact that the baskets of our lives are lovingly woven with the Weaver's touch!

Thank you for joining me on this journey!

When I started my blog in 2012, I thought that it would be a short-term solution for sharing updates with my family and friends regarding my journey through a major life change. Gradually, the readership began to grow outside the sphere of that initial group, and the purpose, scope, and reach of the blog grew as well.

This book, *Petals from the Basket: Devotional Thoughts for Women*, is comprised of some of the favorite blog posts from the website by the same name (www.PetalsfromtheBasket.com). The posts are in no specific order, because life happens in that same way: we can't categorize everything into neat little compartments; and as much as we would like to, we don't always move forward.

Each devotional is followed by a few blank lines on which you may wish to write your own thoughts on the subject or to write out your own prayer of response. However, if you're a perfectionist like I am, you will feel the need to fill every line and to use perfectly shaped handwriting to do so. But I'm giving you permission to leave some (or all) of the lines blank and to simply use them if and when you wish to write in your own thoughts! If I've learned anything from writing these blog posts, it's that nothing is accomplished when it's merely done to "appear perfect." Without sincerity and the freedom to acknowledge our weaknesses, it's difficult to grow stronger.

So as you read through these devotionals, you'll see that I posted them at various times of the year, from different locations, and for different reasons. But my heart's desire is that the thoughts that point you to the unchanging, reliable, consistent truth of God's Word will encourage you, strengthen you, comfort you, teach you, and meet a need that you have at that given moment.

Thank you for walking this journey with me! I'd love to hear from you (petalsfromthebasket@gmail.com), and I'd love for you to visit the blog (www.petalsfromthebasket.com)!

CHALKBOARDS AND CHANGES

A little over two years ago, I began a new job and moved into a new apartment in a new location. *New* was clearly the key word. One of my favorite new purchases after moving was a fourteen-inch, square, gray-and-black-framed chalkboard that now hangs on the wall in my bathroom. I have never written on it. Not once. It's a clean slate. Literally.

Two of my favorite verses in the Bible are found in Lamentations 3:22 and 23 (NLT): *"The faithful love of the Lord never ends! His mercies never cease. Great is His faithfulness; His mercies begin afresh each morning."* So there is something about the visual reminder of that "clean slate" every day that reminds me that God gives me brand new mercies each morning! How amazing is *that?* Actually, since that is a totally rhetorical question, I'm going to write it again and end it like I mean it: How amazing is THAT!

One week ago today, my life went pear-shaped (i.e., the bottom fell out), and I find that I will once again begin a new job, in a new apartment, in a new location. Change. But a change appointed by my unchanging God.

A few moments ago I walked from one side of my apartment to the other and dropped off some freshly folded towels in the bathroom. As I turned to leave, I glanced up at the never-touched-by-chalk chalkboard on the wall. I stopped to wipe away tears of joy as I thanked Him that I'm facing each new day—each change—with fresh mercy!

And that is precisely why, when I move to a new apartment to start a new job in a new location, I will once again hang my clean slate smack-dab in the center of my bathroom wall. After all, not everything needs to change!

This post first appeared on PetalsfromtheBasket.com on March 26, 2012.

I WANT TO LIVE WHERE I CAN
MAKE A DIFFERENCE

I want to live where I can make a difference. That thought struck me early this morning as I wearily rose from my overnight duty in assisting with my dad's care. It's pouring buckets and buckets and buckets of rain in Indiana this morning, and the heavy cloud cover is enveloping me with the realities of fall's presence and winter's approach. All I could think of was moving to a warm climate by a quiet body of water where the only sounds other than those from the nature that surrounded me would be from my fountain pen as it glides across the page in a well-worn leather journal. But in waxing eloquent, I digress!

In fact, my thoughts on living where I can make a difference had nothing to do with my physical location. They came from a recent conversation with someone who lives in the past. You know the type: they frequently relive the "glory days" or bitterness-producing moments of times gone by—times that they can't seem to let go of for one reason or another. Generally, these individuals hang on to the thrill, adulation, or victory of a momentous event. Or perhaps they hold on to a disappointment, a tragedy, or a loss that left a permanent mark on their personal timeline.

In their proper place and when viewed from the right perspective, these events, feelings, or life-changing moments can be amazing memories that serve to shape today into a better day than it might have been otherwise. As learning tools and character-molding opportunities, even the worst human events can create a positive forward momentum.

But here's what struck me by way of reminder and as an "aha" moment today: if I want to make a difference, I have to live in the present, where I have the ability to change and to create change. At the risk of appearing vain, let me repeat that:

If I want to make a difference, I have to live in the present,
where I have the ability to change and to create change.

I can't make a difference in the past. History cannot be changed. But I can make a difference today, and in doing so, I am on my way to making a difference tomorrow—and in each tomorrow that God gives to me.

I think that we often relive the past because its outcome is certain. We don't know what the outcomes of today or tomorrow will be, and maybe you're more secure than I am, but quite honestly, not knowing the outcome of something is scary to me.

Today my reading was from Proverbs 3, which is home to two verses that are familiar to many:

Trust in the Lord with all your heart;
do not depend on your own understanding.
Seek his will in all you do,
and he will show you which path to take.

—Proverbs 3:5–6, NLT

I not only get to make a difference today, but I don't have to consume my thoughts with what will happen there: "He will show [me] which path to take!"

And it is on the path that He has chosen for me that I will get to make a difference.

This post first appeared on PetalsfromtheBasket.com on October 3, 2014.

WHO I AM

I was reading a short devotional this morning as part of my God-and-I Time, and the final phrase stuck out to me: "May who I am glorify You!" It wouldn't leave my mind, and it has, in these few short hours, become the prayer of my heart. "May who I am glorify You." Not who I was or who I wish I were or who I plan to be—but who I *am*.

Each day, each thought, each action—who I *am*. Not when I'm retired, when I'm financially settled, or when I'm married—who I *am*. When I'm famous, when I have time, when I achieve a desired status? No—who I *am*. When I'm thinner, when I'm able to control my desires, when I'm able to live a disciplined life? Again: no—who I *am*.

Lord, hear and help me to live out the sincerity behind this prayer: "May who I *am* glorify You."

_____

_____

_____

_____

This post first appeared on PetalsfromtheBasket.com on November 24, 2014.

THE TRUTH ABOUT RELATIONSHIPS

A standard disclaimer is necessary for this post: I'm not, in any way, shape, or form, a relationship expert. In fact, I'm writing about relationships, and I'm a single, never-been-married woman who is content with being whatever God wants me to be today. To say that my life belongs to Him and then pine over what I don't have or over what I think I want is to say that He's doing something wrong. So I've decided that I can whine until I'm purple in the face (in which case, I come home to an empty house *and* I have a purple face, which is highly unattractive), or I can be the best me that I'm supposed to be today. I make it a daily practice to choose the latter.

This past spring, my niece loaned me a great book: *Relationships: A Mess worth Making*, by Timothy S. Lane and Paul David Tripp. When you finish reading this post, please, please, please either get this for your Kindle or order the hard copy. My standard M.O. with most relationships—from friends, to family, to dating—is to begin with more gusto than I should and then run if anything gets "messy." I had set this book aside several times, but I finally read it all the way through, and I found it to cover all kinds of relationships, all kinds of relevant Scriptures, and all kinds of examples that I'm pretty certain were based on secret notes that all my friends, family members, and past boyfriends sent to the authors. Wow! But the pain was worth it. Even though I've already blown it big time within the last two weeks, I was reminded that grace is a necessary element of every relationship!

The book I'm in the process of reading right now is a book that I won through a contest held by the author, Mary DeMuth. I logged into Twitter one night and saw a note about the contest, completed my entry, and found out two days later that I had won—and it was truly a win! *The Wall around Your Heart: How Jesus Heals You When Others Hurt You* is side-by-side with *Relationships: A Mess worth Making* as one of the best reads I've had in a long time. Again, I have recently failed miserably at applying these principles, but the truths will knock your socks off, and I'm eager for God's grace to provide future opportunities for application. As a woman who goes all-out in what she does, it's easy for relationships to consume me, taking the place of my wonderful God. So the arrow that took the form of the following quotation from Mary DeMuth hit me between the eyes and went straight to my heart when I read it yesterday:

> The more we place expectations on people, the more idolatrous they become in our lives. We serve a jealous God who will not allow us to worship people over Him. Sometimes He moves our relationships in painful ways to remind us of this truth.

Because of several major changes taking place in my life, I've thought about my relationships (with friends, family, etc.) a lot lately—perhaps even over thinking them. Oddly, I kept thinking that I needed to align my thoughts on loving these individuals based on the oft-quoted I Corinthians 13 (which, indeed, should be the goal). I admit with red face that when I tried that, I felt like a failure. (Love is patient—I'm not, so therefore, I must not know how to truly love others, so why bother; love believes all things—I too often believe what I wish rather than what is true, so once again, I have not made it through the filter of this perfect standard.) For me, personally, I have actually found that I Corinthians

13 is a good relationship chapter, but Philippians 4:8 is a *great* relationship verse!

> And now, dear brothers and sisters, one final thing. Fix your thoughts on what is true, and honorable, and right, and pure, and lovely, and admirable. Think about things that are excellent and worthy of praise.
>
> —Philippians 4:8, NLT

Instead of letting my mind filter its thoughts through what-ifs, if-onlys, "I'll bet this is what he's thinking," or "I'm sure this is what she's doing," I must stop to think on what I know to be true. For example, while on a long-distance call with a friend, what if she says that she needs to hang up because something needs her attention, and she says she'll call me back later that afternoon? By 6:30 p.m., she still hasn't called. What is true is simply this: she didn't call me back when she implied that she would. But my sin-prone mind begins to entertain thoughts like: She must be mad at me. She must not want to spend time talking with me after all. She must have lied to me just to get me off the phone. Those are not relationship-building thoughts. Those are negative, influenced-by-the-world-around-me thoughts that don't align with Scripture.

Additionally, when thinking about others, we are to think on things that are honorable, right, pure, lovely, admirable, excellent, and worthy of praise. Do I think about the admirable traits in others, or do I dwell on what I think they've done wrong? (This does, in fact, line up with the love ruler in I Corinthians 13, which states that love doesn't keep account of the wrongs it has suffered. People mess up. Love keeps moving forward.) One response is based on truth; the other, on reactions to unmet expectations.

So, using one of my favorite phrases, I'm going to "bottom line it, baby." Relationships aren't easy—at any level. But they're worth it. And that, my friend, is the truth.

This post first appeared on PetalsfromtheBasket.com on January 12, 2014.

HOW TO LIVE YOUR BIG WHY

A few years ago, my chiropractor at the time was helping me toward greater wellness—principles that, when I applied them, worked well (which is why I've returned to applying them again)! Before we began, however, he had me come up with my "big why."

Just in case you're unfamiliar with that term, it's basically a short, concisely worded, "life-mission-statement-type" answer to the question: What's your long-term motivation?

Knowing the answer to your "big why" guides you in every area of decision making: If it doesn't propel you toward the "big why," don't do it. If it moves you forward on the path toward living out your "big why," do it!

I actually chose a Bible verse to summarize my personal "big why." After hearing Nancy Leigh DeMoss use this verse in a similar manner, I chose John 17:4, a verse that quotes a prayer that Jesus Himself prayed as He looked back on His life:

> "I glorified You on the earth, having accomplished the work which You have given Me to do" (John 17:4, NASB).

This verse is what propels my right choices (though, I often make wrong ones when I don't keep the "big why" and the big picture in view). This verse and this thought remind me that no matter what vocation, relationship, location, or action I may be presented with, it needs to be filtered through this "big why." If I can glorify God by the manner in which I produce the outcome and through the outcome itself, then it's a "go." If not, I must not allow myself to be distracted by it or to be deterred from living out my personal "big why."

Though I'm only on John 8 today in my pre-Easter reading of the Book of John, I was reminded of the "big why" principle that guided Christ as He walked through the ups and downs that His life on earth presented Him.

In John 8, Jesus was telling the angry, unbelieving crowd around Him Who He was—not to "defend" Himself (He had nothing to prove!) but because Who He was (and is!) meant that He could set them free from the sins that enslaved their hearts.

Every thought, every word, every action, every motivation for Christ was for the purpose of giving glory to God and being obedient to God. In John 8:28 (NASB), He said, "I do nothing on my own initiative, but I speak these things as the Father taught me." Every step He took, He took under that guidance of God, allowing Him to live out His "big why," which was to accomplish the work that God gave Him to do.

So what does that look like for my life and your life today? How do we live out our personal "big why?"

1. Determine your personal "big why."

You can't live it out your "big why" if you don't have one! Select a concisely worded, specific, measurable, attainable summary for why you do what you do. You might actually have several little "big whys": one for work, one for relationships, one for your finances, etc. But the one to start with is the one that will be the overall motivating factor for all areas of your life—the one that encompasses everything!

I must add here that this should be your "big why," not what your mama or your daddy or your friends or your boss or anyone else chooses for you (though, of course, the input of their wisdom in your life is invaluable when making major life choices). If your motivation is pleasing others rather than doing what God skilled you to do, in the end, you will most likely fail at accomplishing what you're here to do. Period.

2. Write down your "big why" and memorize it.

Though determining your "big why" is good, having it well-established in your heart and mind (and written in a prominent location where you can easily reference it when needed) will make it more likely for you to actually apply it to your life choices.

3. Begin to apply your "big why" to all of your choices—both large and small!

Should I apply for this job? ("Will it help me to accomplish my 'big why'?") Should I continue in this relationship? ("Will it help me to accomplish my 'big why'?") Should I make this choice in this moment? ("Will it help me to accomplish my 'big why'?")

Though at first it sounds confining to have to filter every single thing you do through some "out there" reason for doing it or not doing it, it's actually very freeing. If it doesn't propel you forward, you know the answer is "no," and you get to move on without wasting valuable moments of a quickly fleeting life on something that will rob you of time, energy, and joy because it's not helping you to accomplish your overall motivating factor! But if it is moving you toward what motivates you, you'll not be constrained with worry, the need to please anyone but God by your choice, or fear of whether or not you should be investing time, energy, and resources into the decision you've made!

I encourage you to take a few minutes today to take action on these three simple—though potentially life-altering—steps and start (or continue) living out your personal "big why!"

Lord, in my secular work, in my sacred work; in my home, outside my home; in my thoughts, in the words and actions they produce may I choose to be guided by a desire to give You glory by the motivation behind it all!

This post first appeared on PetalsfromtheBasket.com on April 8, 2014.

THE POWERFUL TRUTH OF 41414

Numbers intrigue me. I love their unique patterns, and I often form numerical equations in my mind to help me remember things: for example, several years ago, I had a phone number that ended in 1339, which, for a "numbers person" make total sense: 1 x 3 = 3, and 3 x 3 = 9. If you're not a numbers person, you're saying, "huh?" and if you *are* a numbers person, you're thinking, "duh." Any numbers I hear—ever—go through this process! [By the way: all numbers this week (actually, 4/11-19/14) are the same forward and backward: 4/14/14; 4/15/14; 4/16/14, etc.!]

Now that I've let you in on a glimpse of just one odd side of how my mind works (yes, one of many, I'm sure!), you'll understand my fascination with the fact that as I prepared to read John 14 this morning and first asked for God's guidance to point me toward a verse, section, principle, or thought to put into action today, I was led to verse fourteen:

> John 14:14, NASB: "If you ask Me anything in my name, I will do it."

Now, lest you think I'm saying it was some "sign" because of the numbers, I'm not. I'm just sharing that it was cool that after I was pointed toward this verse, the irony of the "numerical fascination" made me smile: John is the fourth book of the New Testament; therefore, my verse of application today was 4/14:14; and today is 4/14/14! Again, it has no spiritual significance—it was just a fun nonessential fact about a very essential verse.

So many religious leaders and groups have turned this verse into what is dubbed the "prosperity Gospel" (the bottom line with that way of thinking is most often: love Jesus and be filthy rich) that we often shy away from its powerful truth.

It's not written in some difficult-to-understand code of numerical (in)significance. Jesus says, "I will do it." Not "I might"; not, "I'll think about it." He says, "I will do it." And He keeps His word.

So, because Jesus keeps His word, is my faith so small that I am not receiving what I ask, or am I receiving what I ask, but my faith is so small that I can't see it?"

Lord, my relationship with You too often runs so shallow that I impose my own thoughts and reactions onto You. Yet I come to You today with a sense of longing, imploring You to grant my desire for renewed fellowship and for You to answer, "I will do it." Lord, I want to know You—not the You I imagine You to be, based on my finite thoughts, but the You Who keeps His word and supersedes those expectations by more than I could ever ask or think.

This post first appeared on PetalsfromtheBasket.com on, of course, April 14, 2014.

REJOICE…IN THE LORD

For more than twenty years, I have used the Inductive Bible Study Method taught by Kay Arthur and Precept Ministries. Part of this method includes marking key words (using symbols and colors) as you read and study the Bible. (I won't take time to teach the Precept method; you can read more about it on their site: www.precept.org.)

One of the symbols I habitually use is for the words *joy* and *rejoice*. When those words appear within a passage or verse that I am reading, I place a smiley face and a heart over the word. The very first time I marked the word joy, I simply used a smiley face; however, I returned to that verse a few minutes later to add the heart next to it. I believe that being joyful is not about being happy; it is about being happy in my heart—where circumstances, situations, and even people cannot reach in and steal that level of calm, steady, sincere happiness.

Last night, I read Habakkuk 3:17–18, and I think these verses summarize it clearly (emphasis mine):

> Though the fig tree does not bud
> and there are no grapes on the vines,
> though the olive crop fails
> and the fields produce no food,
> though there are no sheep in the pen
> and no cattle in the stalls,

yet *I will rejoice in the Lord,*
I will be joyful in God my Savior."

—Habakkuk 3:17–18 (NIV)

In the middle of many difficulties and trials, the writer states without wavering that he will nevertheless rejoice in the Lord. He is not "happy in spite of the circumstances"; he is rejoicing "in the Lord."

There are nine verses that use the exact phrase: "rejoice in the Lord." (I used the KJV for looking up this phrase on the Internet, using www.BibleGateway.com for this post.) If you have a moment today, take to read them and be reminded that our joy comes not in what or who is around us. True joy—lasting, sincere joy—comes from one place: in the Lord!

1. Psalm 33:1
   "Rejoice in the Lord, O ye righteous: for praise is comely for the upright."
2. Psalm 97:12
   "Rejoice in the Lord, ye righteous; and give thanks at the remembrance of his holiness."
3. Isaiah 41:16
   "Thou shalt fan them, and the wind shall carry them away, and the whirlwind shall scatter them: and thou shalt rejoice in the Lord, and shalt glory in the Holy One of Israel."
4. Isaiah 61:10
   "I will greatly rejoice in the Lord, my soul shall be joyful in my God; for he hath clothed me with the garments of salvation, he hath covered me with the robe of righteousness, as a bridegroom decketh himself with ornaments, and as a bride adorneth herself with her jewels."
5. Joel 2:23
   "Be glad then, ye children of Zion, and rejoice in the Lord your God: for he hath given you the former rain moderately, and he

will cause to come down for you the rain, the former rain, and the latter rain in the first month."

6. Habakkuk 3:18
   "Yet I will rejoice in the Lord, I will joy in the God of my salvation."

7. Zechariah 10:7
   "And they of Ephraim shall be like a mighty man, and their heart shall rejoice as through wine: yea, their children shall see it, and be glad; their heart shall rejoice in the Lord."

8. Philippians 3:1
   "Finally, my brethren, rejoice in the Lord. To write the same things to you, to me indeed is not grievous, but for you it is safe."

9. Philippians 4:4
   "Rejoice in the Lord always: and again I say, Rejoice."

This post first appeared on PetalsfromtheBasket.com on June 4, 2013.

THE CHANGE I DESIRE MOST

My address is changing. My hairstyle just changed—again. My plans have changed. The current eight-week theme at my new church is about change. My goals have changed. My desires have changed. It's clearly a season of change. Yet in the midst of outward change, I'm finding that the most important change of all is not around me. In fact, it's not even the changes *about* me. The most important change of all is the change that I desire to have *within* me:

> An all-encompassing love for God; a greater eagerness to follow Him than to lead others; a sincere contentment in His plan, in His time, and in His way; a commitment to Him that won't waver; a prayer life that weaves my heart together with God's heart; a longing for Him above all others; and a hunger for His Word that transforms my heart beyond recognition.

Lord, change me.

_____

_____

_____

This post first appeared on PetalsfromtheBasket.com on February 18, 2014.

THE TUESDAY AFTER THE WEDDING

My sister Karen was the first of my siblings to get married. (I'm the youngest of four children.) I remember someone telling my mom to cancel all her plans for the Tuesday after Karen's Saturday wedding—because she would most likely be sick that day. Say what?

Apparently, the mother of the bride is often sick on the Tuesday after a weekend wedding. Possible reasons are: the exhaustion catches up with her; the extreme high of the excitement has nowhere to go but down; or it could be that she finally has *time* to get sick! She's been so busy with wedding preparation, the wedding day, and returning rented and borrowed items in the midst of saying farewells to visiting family members that she hasn't had time to stop. When she does, it hits, and she is totally wiped out—and gets sick.

So often after a big event, there is a time when all the buildup of the event comes to a screeching halt, and the reality of reality sets in. Yes, this can happen after a joyful wedding, but it can also happen following a major loss.

Sadly (and I have no scientific proof or statistics to back this up), I also think that Tuesday—or the equivalent number of days following a major event—is the day when most people stop praying for the friend or loved one going through that celebration or that time of saying final goodbyes. We go on with our lives—go back to work, fill out our to-do lists, and prepare for the next event—but we forget that their lives are now drastically different. In both cases, celebrating and mourning, something is now missing, and the emptiness becomes louder as the words of encouragement grow fainter.

So today, I encourage you to think of someone who has recently celebrated or of someone who has recently lost a loved one and determine to make Tuesdays a day when you think of and pray for friends or loved ones who have had major life changes recently.

Here are some simple ideas for reaching out:

1. Call your friend today and plan something for next Tuesday. It doesn't have to cost a penny! Ask her to go on a 30-minute walk with you; invite her for coffee from 9:30–10:30 a.m. (at that time of day, you only need coffee and a muffin—or even just coffee); or invite her to join you to go pick out the flowers for your new flower bed.

2. Send a card in the mail on Saturday so that it is likely to arrive at your friend's home on Tuesday. Just let her know that you're praying for her and share a favorite verse or a lesson that God has been teaching you lately.

3. Call her on Tuesday and tell her that you're praying for her. You can literally call and say, "I'm not going to keep you long— I called for one thing only: I just wanted you to know I'm praying for you today. I'll call you later in the week to see if we can get together for coffee soon, but for today, just know that I'm praying for you." That's it. But do it on a Tuesday.

4. I have a friend who lost her son on the twelfth day of the month. I have written in my calendar for the next six months (and I might extend it if it seems right to do so) to send a card on the ninth of each month so that when it arrives at her home on the twelfth, she will simply be encouraged by knowing that I

haven't forgotten that her ache is very real—and that God's everlasting arms are still holding her in the midst of it. It might not be on a Tuesday, and it will take effort on my part, but the point is to be intentional about demonstrating ongoing love and concern for those who celebrate and for those who grieve.

"Rejoice with them that do rejoice, and weep with them that weep" (Romans 12:15, KJV).

Oh, and if you've read this far down, you deserve to know: my mom got sick on the Tuesday following Karen's wedding.

This post first appeared on PetalsfromtheBasket.com on May 23, 2013.

HOLDING UP THE POSTER BOARD

Do you have a life verse: one that summarizes your purpose or perhaps carries great meaning because of the life-changing impact it had on you? You know by now that I don't do anything the "normal way!" While it's true that I have a "life verse," I actually have two additional verses that I claim under that heading.

First of all, I have a "life" verse—thanks to Dr. Jack Wyrtzen. He sat in our living room one night and taught me the importance of a life verse—using this one (he told me it was his own life verse) as the example. I use this verse to remind me that all that I do is not being done for the acceptance of people; instead, it should be done to the glory of God.

"So whether you eat or drink or whatever you do, do it all for the glory of God." —I Corinthians 10:31, NIV

Believe it or not, I also have a "death" verse. Yup, you read that right! Thanks to the influence of Miss Nancy Leigh DeMoss, the verse I long to be able to say when my time of death comes is the one Christ spoke prior to His sacrificial death on my behalf.

"I have brought you glory on earth by completing the work you gave me to do." — John 17:4, NIV

My final verse is a "verse for the year." This one, obviously, changes each year. I usually choose it because it seems to be a God-given direction for the year ahead. Sadly, February arrived without my having chosen my annual "verse for the year." I was honestly a little troubled that nothing seemed to be the one I felt God would have me to focus on. However, today in church, my pastor closed the service with the verse that hit straight into the middle of my heart! I wanted to stand up and hold up a poster board with the words, "WOO HOO!" (Don't panic. I didn't—not externally, anyhow!) So I acknowledge Pastor Chip Bernhard as the one God used to influence the selection of this year's verse.

"Ah, Sovereign Lord, you have made the heavens and the earth by your great power and outstretched arm. Nothing is too hard for you." —Jeremiah 32:17, NIV

This post first appeared on PetalsfromtheBasket.com on February 3, 2013.

A BONUS LESSON FROM MARY AND MARTHA

The names Mary and Martha are often spoken as one word, MaryandMartha, because the mention of their names takes us to the true and familiar story in the Bible that talks about the contrast in their "learning styles." As their contrast is emphasized—often through books, Bible study lessons, and speakers at ladies' retreats—we are challenged to sadly acknowledge that we are often "Marthas"; yet, we long to be more like Mary.

Theirs was a lesson God probably chose to include so we could see that while serving Christ is great, truly knowing Him is better. (Later, take time to read Luke 10:38–42.)

However, while reading another historical record that speaks of these two sisters—found in John 11:1–45—it hit me that in this lesson, both sisters demonstrated an awesome focus; although, their focus here is often mistaken as we hurriedly read to check off "God-and-I-Time" on our daily to-do lists.

In this passage, Lazarus, the brother of Mary and Martha and a close friend of Jesus, died. While the fact that Jesus raised Lazarus from the dead is clearly the primary focus of this passage, note the response by Martha and the identical response by her sister, Mary:

Martha's response, verse 21, NIV: "Lord…if You had been here, my brother would not have died."

Mary's response, verse 32, NIV: "Lord, if You had been here, my brother would not have died."

Perhaps it's due to our natural, sinful, negative tendencies, but at first glance, we often read those as "accusatory" statements from the sisters. However, look closely. Do you see it? It's an incredible "bonus" lesson God provided for us from these two often-contrasted but now identical personalities.

Look at the faith represented by those mirrored comments! Both Martha and Mary acknowledged the great power that they knew Christ had! His very presence could have prevented what seemed horrid. Perhaps it was not that they were not accusing Him of "neglect," but that they were demonstrating that now they both truly knew the magnitude of His power and had an understanding that He was able because He was Lord of all!

Maybe, when all is said and done, we can say with gratitude that we not only want to be like Mary, but we also want to be like Martha after all.

_____

_____

_____

_____

_____

_____

This post first appeared on PetalsfromtheBasket.com on September 9, 2013.

GIMME THAT GARMET-GRABBING FAITH

In reading through the twenty-four chapters of the Book of Luke between December 1 and 24, I have once again been overwhelmed by reading about the miracles of Christ. I'll confess that while I am amazed by His actions, I am saddened by my own.

I see what He has done, and I see Him at work in my life, yet I neglect to trust Him fully. I find myself distracted by the things of this world that cause me to waver in the kind of faith I want to have.

In Luke 8, the true story is told of a woman who had been ill for twelve years with no relief. Jesus came to town, and she went to see Him. She had undoubtedly heard of His miracles and was eager to experience one first-hand—literally!

In my mind's eye, the crowd was pushing in on her, and she seemed to know that ducking down low to push her way through them was her only chance at getting close enough to be healed. I can imagine that she reached out—only to have her fingers nearly trampled by those surrounding the Great Teacher. She tried again. This time she reached for all she was worth. She knew that just a touch was all she needed—at least, that's all it took to heal the blind man who lived down the road from her.

This time, her outstretched arm succeeded in its quest: she touched the hem of the robe that Jesus was wearing! Without any word from the Master, she felt the effects of the healing that had instantaneously occurred. However, now she was faced with having to answer His question—"Who touched me?"—in front of everyone. Peter tried to tell Him that it was just the crowd that was pressing in on Him, but He again said: "Someone touched me; I know that power has gone out from me."

Luke 7:47–48 (NIV) gives us the conclusion to her story: "Then the woman, seeing that she could not go unnoticed, came trembling and fell at His feet. In the presence of all the people, she told why she had touched Him and how she had been instantly healed. Then he said to her, 'Daughter, your faith has healed you. Go in peace.'"

This has been a lengthy post, but I want to share three quick things I learned/am learning from this woman's faith.

She came with reckless abandon. Nothing else mattered but getting to Jesus. She was willing to drop to her knees and crawl if that's what it took!

She reached out to Him. She opened her empty, weak hand and persisted until she had received what only He could give.

She revered His power. Her trembling acknowledgment that she was the one who had touched Him demonstrated her reverent awe of His holiness and her respect for the fact that this was the Great Physician. I believe that it is in acknowledging our belief in His power that we receive His power!

However, my three alliterated points mean nothing if I don't put them into practice in 2012…and beyond. Therefore, I must apply these three principles to my own faith:

*Come to Him in reckless abandon, taking no care for the distractions that come

*Reach out to the One Who is able to do exceeding abundantly above all that I could ever ask or think

*Have a reverent respect ("the fear of the Lord") for how incredibly awesome and powerful He is

In applying these principles, I will be able to add a fourth *r* by "rejoicing" in all that He does in me, through me, and for me! Oh, how I long for a garment-grabbing faith!

This post first appeared on PetalsfromtheBasket.com on December 13, 2012.

FREEZER FOR RENT

Actually, there are no longer any vacancies in my freezer, but not too long ago, I could have hung that sign on the front of it! Losing my job six months ago brought about changes and blessings I never expected when driving home from my last day of work. Yet, truly knowing that my God is sovereign and loving and caring and in control and—well, *so* much more than even *that*—I truly had this heaven-sent knowledge that His way was perfect!

I hesitate sharing stories that sound like I'm crying "poor me" or making life all about money, but I trust that you will read the following true events and see in them the full hand of God pouring out its riches into my very empty hands. And by riches, I don't mean a full bank account, a new car, or any "earthly luxuries" that might come to mind when you read that word. I mean *true* riches!

My previous work was for a nonprofit organization. Because of that, I was not able to receive unemployment during the months I was looking for work. For many, unemployment can provide much-needed resources for maintaining life's basics during the time of transition. However, the majority of churches and other nonprofit, faith-based organizations do not pay into unemployment, so I could not receive any of the benefits from that program.

Because I spent almost four months looking diligently 24/7 for full-time salaried employment and ended with zero results, I came before the Lord and asked Him to help me get work using the talents and abilities He has entrusted to me. It was at that point that I began PEP Writing Services so that I can freelance or do contract work using my training and skills in proofreading and editing. Some weeks I work 30 hours; some, only two. Any business or freelance/contract work takes time to build, and so I continue my pursuit of additional clients and more steady means of necessary income.

To say the least, things got lean. I determined, however, that since God had clearly allowed the event to occur, He would be faithful in providing for its resulting outcome. Again, please note that I write this *only* to praise the One Who is Jehovah-Jireh! I have clothing, food, shelter, and more, and I consider myself blessed beyond measure!

I am writing this particular post to share three specific, very personal but true, wonderful things in praise to the One Who provides in hopes that they will encourage others. Yes, He prompted human instruments to care for the physical aspects of these, but I know by the specific answers that He was the Ultimate Provider:

1. I needed a new computer program for my home computer. I had used the program at my previous office, and now I was without the much-needed program for preparing my resume, cover letters, etc. The cost was $150.00 to purchase this suite of programs, and an extra $150.00 was nowhere to be found. I prayed on Wednesday morning, telling the Lord I would not ask anyone for money, but that I was trusting Him to supply this, because it was truly a necessity. Two hours later I went to the mailbox and found a gift from some dear friends—for $150.00. I praised Him for answering so quickly, and then realized, no, He kept His Word and answered before I asked—they mailed it on Monday!

2. Another very specific need for $100.00 arose. A need, not a want. Same thing as before. Exact amount. Mailed three days before I asked Him to provide.

3. Food has at times become a "luxury item" over the last few months. Yes, I have the necessities, but I will humbly and honestly share that there were a couple of mornings when I opened a can of green beans and carefully divided it into three bowls—one for breakfast, one for lunch, and one for supper. Again, I don't share this as a "poor me" but only to relay to you what God has done, is doing, and will continue to do! A couple of weeks ago, I received a gift of frozen meats that the giver had precooked and prepacked into one-person servings. It was enough to fill an entire large Coleman cooler! As I have had a *very* busy week of editing (another *huge* provision of work from the Lord), I have cried tears of joy with each packet I have removed from the freezer and have thawed to have for a ready-made healthful lunch or supper! Therefore, there is no more need for a "Freezer for Rent" sign to be hung! Instead, the door of my freezer holds a Post-it note that reads: Jehovah-Jireh (God, my Provider)!

He keeps His Word. That's the bottom line. In Matthew 6:25–33, He reminds me that I am to put Him first. The rest is up to Him to provide for because He can, He does, and He will!

> "Therefore I tell you, do not worry about your life, what you will eat or drink; or about your body, what you will wear. Is not life more than food, and the body more than clothes? Look at the birds of the air; they do not sow or reap or store away in barns, and yet your heavenly Father feeds them. Are you not much more valuable than they? Can any one of you by worrying add a single hour to your life? "And why do you worry about clothes? See how the flowers of the field grow. They do not labor or spin. Yet I tell you that not even Solomon in all his splendor was dressed like one of

these. If that is how God clothes the grass of the field, which is here today and tomorrow is thrown into the fire, will he not much more clothe you—you of little faith? So do not worry, saying, 'What shall we eat?' or 'What shall we drink?' or 'What shall we wear?' For the pagans run after all these things, and your heavenly Father knows that you need them. But seek first his kingdom and his righteousness, and all these things will be given to you as well" (NIV).

This post first appeared on PetalsfromtheBasket.com on September 21, 2012.

WISDOM FROM THE ROCKING CHAIR

Knowing my love for antiques, a friend recently gave me her grandmother's rocking chair. There's something about a rocking chair that produces thoughts of wise elderly women rocking back and forth and knitting or crocheting as they exude more wisdom with every stitch. I often wish I could sit at the feet of these women as they speak the knowledge they have gained from their many years on earth and from the experiences that resulted in the wisdom they are able to share.

Learning from others is critical to our own growth as individuals. The wealth of information available to us is increasing with every page we read from biographies, every article we read online, every Facebook status, every blog post, every tweet, and so on. So why, and again I ask, why, would we not avail ourselves of every opportunity to learn from others?

The answer? I believe that our pride makes us think that we are worthy of nothing less than being teachers; therefore, we naturally shy away from admitting our need to remain students, even as we teach. I may not like everything a teacher/writer/blogger does, but I want to learn what I can from his or her experience, wisdom ,and knowledge, add in my God-focused philosophy of life, and be better off for having learned what they were able to teach.

Let me quickly add that I believe that we can learn *something* from everyone—even if it is merely becoming stronger in our own beliefs by learning that we don't want to be like them or follow their teachings at all! But the important thing is to approach each person, each day, and each experience as though they were lessons from which to learn.

However, humility of heart is required, for in placing ourselves under the teaching of another, we are admitting that we have not yet achieved perfection!

This desire to learn from others is prevalent in the Bible in the life of Joshua. His numerous references to all that Moses taught him demonstrate humility, gratitude, and a teachable spirit that formed him into a great national leader. Though appointed by God Himself, Joshua respected the wisdom Moses had gained from following God. Joshua clearly intended to honor Moses—and God!—by applying that knowledge to his own life and to his leadership of God's people. [I encourage you to read the Book of Joshua and note all the references to the teachings of Moses!]

No matter our biological age, there will be times when we are called upon to sit in the rocking chair and times when we will have opportunities to sit at the feet of others in the rocking chair. May we be willing to view both through the eyes of opportunity and with a heart of humility for the unique set of privileges that they hold.

_____

_____

_____

_____

_____

This post first appeared on PetalsfromtheBasket.com on September 11, 2012.

SO HE MADE IT OVER

"But the pot he was shaping from the clay was marred in his hands; so the potter formed it into another pot, shaping it as seemed best to him" (Jeremiah 18:4, NIV).

The Amplified Bible says, "So He made it over."

"So He made it over." I am not disposable to God! He has placed a value on me (through the blood of Christ) that will never diminish! So when I am "marred," He chooses to remake me: perhaps for a different use or purpose or with an updated design or function, but He doesn't dispose of me!

Oh the blessed intermingling of grace and hope!

_____

_____

_____

_____

_____

This post first appeared on PetalsfromtheBasket.com on November 17, 2014.

I'M THANKFUL FOR THE DAY THAT NEVER WAS

"Any regrets I may have over that which I have lost are swallowed up in relief over that which I have escaped." ~Unknown

That quotation has been my annual "mantra" on August 9. However, I take it one step further and use it to realize that it is because of the goodness and wisdom of God that I can view this day in that way.

Some may read what I am about to share and think that I should "be over it by now." I am.

Some may read what I am about to share and think that I am in some way bitter. I am not.

Some may read what I am about to share and think that I must somehow despise men. I do not. Unh-unh, no way, no how!

I'm going to share it anyhow—but not to prove anything or to defend myself against those whose thinking couldn't be further from the truth. I share this because somewhere there is a girl, a family member, a coworker, a friend whose life plans just changed, and I want her to know that she's not the only one, that joy will come again, and that hope will return.

With my wedding plans nearly finalized for my—you guessed it—August 9, 1986 wedding date, I received a call mid-April that changed everything. The wedding was off, and the reality of an uncertain future loomed before me, taunting me with its emptiness and lack of hope. I had cancelled my contract for teaching the following year (and my replacement had already been secured), and there I was, twenty-five years old, with every well-laid-out plan beyond that minute suddenly erased with the giant pink eraser of "there will be no wedding on August ninth."

Before I continue, I will be transparent and tell you that it hurt deeply, and that for several months, when I looked at what I was "missing out on," I was bitter, angry, and, quite honestly, a little ticked off. But when I looked at how God used that one single moment in time to change my life—and my heart—I became grateful, encouraged, and comforted. God knew best. The man to whom I was engaged married not long after, and his wife was the perfect match for him. They faithfully serve the Lord together, and the choice to put an abrupt end to our plans—in the long run and in the big picture—was the right one.

When I was finally able to take the blinders off of my view of things, I saw so clearly that I was in love with love, and he and I both deserved more than that. God's love runs so much deeper than anything we can "muster up" just because we long for marriage.

Sadly, I primarily received the empty platitude from so many people that I had probably even said more than once myself: "God's got someone better in store for you."

First of all, just because he chose not to marry you does not make him a bad person. Though many people use that expression to "console" someone who is sad after a breakup, it's not a great expression. In fact, it's kind of tacky and lame to attack "the bad guy" or "the bad girl."

Secondly, maybe God has singleness, not "someone better," in store for you. But be careful here. Don't follow my poor example of saying (as I did more than once at that time) that "I'm never going to get married.

No one's going to ever hurt me like that again." I feel that I can say this because I'm single, but I can generally recognize the woman who is bitter or desperate because she is so verbal about her singleness—and usually in loud and brash ways, accompanied by sarcasm about the subject. I long to go whisper one simple thing to women like that: "Shh."

Am I tickled pink about not having an earthly life companion? No, I'm not. Am I thrilled to be exactly where God wants me to be at this moment, in this place? You bet I am! Because His way truly is perfect. God didn't bop Himself upside the head that April morning of my phone call and say, "Oh stink, I forgot all about Brenda." He knows what's best for me. He allowed me to learn things that I would never have known otherwise.

So be careful about the "consolation" you give to others:

"It's good to be single. Think of all the things you couldn't do if you were married." "It's better to not be married than to be married to the wrong person."

And on the opposite side, when someone becomes engaged:

"Oh, you'll love married life. Being married is the best thing ever!" "There are so many more ways you can serve as a married couple."

Instead, we as the body of Christ need to joyfully serve in whatever way—at whatever time—God has for us. Perhaps what we should simply say (and what we should simply teach our children and those in the church pews) is:

The best thing you can be is what God wants you to be today, in this moment, in this place. His way is perfect.

When we view life through that lens, we can, with sincerity and a joyful heart, be thankful for the day that never was because it has been a vital part of making us who were are today.

This post first appeared on PetalsfromtheBasket.com on August 9, 2014.

TO BE SILENT OR TO SPEAK UP?

"All that is necessary for the triumph of evil is that good men do nothing." —Edmund Burke

Although this quotation is generally attributed to Edmund Burke, it is found nowhere in his notes. However, many things from the 1700s seem to have disappeared, so maybe that's why no one has found it! But, that's beside the point!

When I read this quotation yesterday, I couldn't help but be a little divided in my reaction to it. Please bear with me through this entire post. I've promised to be transparent, so transparent I shall be—but please don't choose your answer to the title's question until you've read the entire post.

I like the principle behind this quotation. It implies integrity, involvement, intentional choices, and probably a whole bunch of other things that start with the letter *i*. After all, in the United States, one of our greatest privileges is our right to vote—a means of doing something. We have seen over and over again that when citizens fail to speak up with their votes, evil triumphs, and this can happen in any segment of the government and in any region—or even nationally.

Don't panic. This is not a political post—you know that's not my style! However, that scenario paints the picture that would most clearly replicate the thought that comes to mind when reading this familiar quotation. It can be applied to many areas: from schoolyard bullying to international wars; from backyard spats to the overthrow of corrupt governments. Because of this, people often use this quotation and the principles behind it to loudly proclaim the evils of individuals, organizations, or government as a whole.

However (and this is the part that first divided my thinking on this), there is also a time when silence is the loudest weapon you can have and the strongest action you can take. You have heard me share my parents' all-too-often-needed reminder to me that "silence can never be misquoted." Yes, it can be misunderstood, and it can be misinterpreted. But it is important to note that the silence element is the only part that you are responsible for. The misquoting, misunderstanding, and misinterpreting—all of which often lead to misrepresenting!—fall back on the other party. You do not give account for their actions—only your own.

Jesus, the One Whose life we wish to emulate, "opened not His mouth" when evil seemed to be triumphant: the crowds were mocking Him, and Roman soldiers were beating Him. Wow! That wasn't weakness at all! That took tremendous courage, grace, and strength!

Yet, this same Jesus boldly taught against sin and spoke out against evil. His very life on earth was lived so that evil will not be triumphant in the end! (I hope your computer screen just heard a "hallelujah" out of you!)

So, which is it—silence or speaking up? As I read the quotation of wisdom from Edmund Burke and think about the example of Jesus Christ, I believe that the correct answer is: both. Knowing when to use which one becomes a matter of choice based on motivation, circumstance, timing, location, cause, etc. The bottom line is that what I say—either through my words or through my silence—must always be used in order to impact others in a way that allows good to triumph!

Suggested reading:

Psalm 19:14

Isaiah 53

James 3

Philippians 2

This post first appeared on PetalsfromtheBasket.com on February 20, 2013.

THE SOUND OF CONSECRATED FEET

"I'm going to run a marathon one of these days." My friend had said this to me so many times that I'd lost track of the exact number. She reads oodles of books on fitness, she eats well, and she even teaches an occasional course on diet and exercise. After hearing her mention the marathon for the umpteenth time, I wanted to encourage her with, "That's awesome!" However, all I could think was, "Stop talking about it and go do it!" So, being the loving, honest, and caring friend that I am, I said, "Stop talking about it and go do it!"

Last night, I thought of my friend and her annual "one of these days" statements, and I thought, "I am the same annoyance to God that my friend is to me." She had all the tools; she could quote fact after fact and statistic after statistic; and with carefully planned outlines, she could teach others the principles for proper preparation, correct form, healthful diet, and appropriate attire for running long distances. Yet, she had never run a long distance! No wonder I was often annoyed with her (lovingly so) for being so well equipped and not making her knowledge personal by putting feet behind her words (no pun intended).

Yet, here I am, well equipped with all the tools for serving others, able to sing praises to Him, write blog posts, and teach classes on biblical principles that equip others for service—and personally doing so little. No, I've never audibly heard the voice of God, but last night, I heard an inward voice saying, "Stop talking about it and go do it! Put some feet to that praise! Love those that I love…feed my sheep."

So, I just want you to know that I have begun to prepare for a "spiritual marathon." I have a plan in place! I plan to stop talking about it and go do it! No, I'm not headed to Africa—though if that's where God wanted me, that's where I'd go! No, I'm not selling all that I own (all $1.47 worth of it!) to go feed the poor. But I am taking action steps to be intentional about seeking out the lost and the helpless. I hope you'll join me in putting feet—consecrated feet—to our praise!

Suggested reading: John 21: 15–17

This post first appeared on PetalsfromtheBasket.com on February 18, 2013.

BUH-BYE

One of the questions in my Bible study homework for this week was, "How can we 'gird up the loins of our minds'?" It was taken from Peter's instruction in I Peter 1:13, which states (in the King James Version): "Wherefore gird up the loins of your mind, be sober, and hope to the end for the grace that is to be brought unto you at the revelation of Jesus Christ."

To answer the homework question honestly, I had to say: "I need to rid myself of things that distract me from a forward—Godward—focus." It meant changing some things. It meant that the time was now for eliminating distractors!

For me, distractors are usually much scarier than the obvious "bad" things: too much television or reading, too much time on social networking sites, or being lazy. No, for me, the distractors can be good things, like: helping a friend, encouraging someone, participating in a discussion group on Facebook, or even (prepare for what sounds like heresy coming from me) too much time spent in goal setting or developing time-management tools.

So this morning, in obedience to Spirit-inspired, Peter-written instructions from God Himself, I began to get rid of distractors. I unsubscribed to e-mails that have no positive benefit—ever. I moved my work station to the area of my apartment where I am most productive. I made a list of Facebook groups that I will graciously withdraw from today, etc.

I'm actually looking forward to a week of saying "buh-bye" to these distractors and reintroducing myself to those things that serve a "forward-focus" purpose. In doing so, I pray that my mind will have more room for things that matter!

This post first appeared on PetalsfromtheBasket.com on February 4, 2013.

THE JOY OF OVERWHELMING TEARS

I can't believe I cried. There I was: with a godly man whose character, confidence, humor, intelligence, and wisdom intrigued me. And to top it all off, he was cute.

But as I sat across the table from him on our dinner date, I cried.

Now one thing that many who are close to me know about me is that I have an excruciatingly tender heart. I am sentimental, easily touched, and have a disproportionate amount of empathy for others, and, you guessed it, when those emotions come flooding into my heart, the overflow is seen through the tears running down my cheeks. But on a date? (Perhaps that was a contributing factor as to why it was our one and only date, but that's a whole 'nother story that I hope won't distract our focus from what matters in this one!)

What would make me cry so easily in such a setting? It was the fact that these were not tears of sorrow but tears that resulted from being overwhelmed by the goodness of God.

My date had graciously asked various questions about my life, and as I shared much of what had transpired during recent years following my "mandatory resignation," which had led to many months with no significant income, I realized anew the amazing provisions from my almighty God!

After sharing a few of the ways that God had, in His unfailing faithfulness and because of His unconditional love, provided material things—things like groceries, clothing, gas money, and more—and had taught me invaluable lessons about His all-encompassing power, the tears of gratitude began to flow. I said to the compassionate man sitting across from me, "I'm sorry to cry, but He's just been so amazing that I simply have to talk about Him!"

While reading from Psalm 30 this morning, I was reminded of this event and thought to myself: When was the last time my tears of thankfulness to God flowed this freely? When was the last time I could not keep silent? When was the last time my heart was overtaken by overwhelming joy?

I confess right here, right now that I have become distracted by that which is good but that, even in its goodness, turns my heart to the temporal rather than the eternal. And in the process, I, like the children of Israel who so often experienced—and just as often forgot—the blessings of God, have become "unaffected" by His incomparable mercy and grace.

So my public and private prayer today are one and the same: *Lord, unclutter my heart that I might once again stand in awe of who You are in such a way that I cannot help but proclaim it by my words and by my life!*

_____

_____

_____

_____

_____

_____

This post first appeared on PetalsfromtheBasket.com on October 24, 2014.

WHATEVER YOU SAY

Jesus's mother had such a strong belief in Who He was that she confidently told the servants at the wedding in Cana: "Whatever He says to you, do it" (John 2:5, NASB).

Too often—far too often—I say or inwardly imply, "Do what Jesus says—plus this amazing advice that I'm going to add."

When they did what He said, the results were miraculous! In fact, they were the springboard for and initial instance of all of Jesus's earthly miracles!

Lord, strengthen my will and give me the grace to radically do whatever You say.

This post first appeared on PetalsfromtheBasket.com on April 2, 2014.

THE SECURITY OF SILENCE

It was 1982. We had only been dating a few months when my "beau" at the time took me to a basketball game at the college we were both attending. We had a unique relationship right from the start: laughing, talking easily, and never running out of things to learn about each other. But that day, while watching the game, we hit a "first" that threw me for a loop:

Neither of us was saying anything. It was suddenly silent.

My overly naive reaction at that point in our what turned out to be multiple years together was to panic. In fact—and remember: I admitted that I was naive (and did I mention the word emotional?)—I turned my head in the opposite direction and began to get tears in my eyes. The silence continued as he enjoyed the game and enjoyed being with me and as I continued to think that our relationship was now doomed because there was silence, and we had run out of things to say to each other.

As I sincerely tried to be sneaky about wiping away the tears that were gradually finding their way down my cheeks, my beau saw what I was doing and asked me why I was crying. "It's silent. We have nothing to say to each other. And I thought we were going to be together a long time." Bless his dear heart, he didn't laugh, make fun of me, or run away as fast as he could—surprisingly!

He just looked at me, smiled sweetly, and said, "We're finally at the place where we're secure enough to be silent." That's all it took. I was fine; we continued to spend time together and to date for quite a while after that, until God, in His great wisdom for both of us, led us in opposite directions.

But that simple, patiently and tenderly spoken statement has stuck with me all these years.

My loving, patient God speaks that same thought to me often:

"Be still and know that I am God." —Psalm 46:10, NLT

It's as if He looks at me tenderly—in the midst of my naive emotions and moments of panic—and says, "Be secure enough in Me to know that silence is okay, Brenda. I've got this. Find rest, calm, and certainty in the relationship you have with Me." And when I hear those words, I find an unsurpassed security in the silence that demonstrates calm, trust, and hope.

This post first appeared on PetalsfromtheBasket.com on January 17, 2014.

HERE AM I, LORD—I'LL STAY

I have no idea what Hebrew punctuation marks look like or how—or if—they were appropriately translated into the English versions we have of the Bible, but I love the fact that in many of the versions (NIV, NKJV, ESV, NASB, etc.) Isaiah 6:8 contains an exclamation point!

> Then I heard the voice of the Lord saying, "Whom shall I send? And who will go for us?" And I said, "Here am I. Send me!" —Isaiah 6:8, NIV

I will confess that I often stand in surprised wonder at those who are not willing to go wherever God leads or at those—I'm sorry moms and grandmas, but it must be said—who are not willing for their children or grandchildren to go wherever God leads. It just doesn't support our belief in who we say God is when we selfishly cling to people or things in ways and by words that don't live out our teachings that "His way is perfect."

Perhaps because the Lord chose to use my father's ministry as a pastor in several different churches throughout my life, I have this deep-rooted philosophy that "wherever He sends, I'll go." Yes, it's hard to leave behind friends and family at times, and yes, there is a part of me that would love to live in the same place for a very long time, but there is a greater joy in letting God be the One to make those decisions for me (that's the great principle of submission, by the way).

I often say, "I love wherever I am." And I truly do. But I also often add: "But if the Lord said, 'I want you to move to _____ tomorrow,' I'd say, 'Okay,' and I'd start packing."

So when the opportunity or the need arises somewhere, I often say to the Lord—in tones of an elementary-aged student eagerly raising her hand and literally waving it in hopes of being called on by the teacher— "Here am I. Send me!"

For me personally, leaving where I am and heading into a new adventure and a new means of serving Christ is relatively easy. However, that means that, for me anyhow, staying is hard. Maybe it's because the day-in, day-out life of just consistently serving Him requires a discipline that I am still building into my life—little by little and, yes, day by day.

I will share that I was very recently presented with an awesome opportunity to serve in a ministry I love, in an area of the country that I love, and with people that I love. My hand immediately raised, and I began waving my arms in eager anticipation of getting to go—for all the right reasons, I might add.

Yet, as I sought the Lord in Scripture, He continued to show me verses like: "Dwell in the land and cultivate faithfulness." (Psalm 37:3, NASB) In my zealous desire to get to be the one He allowed to fill this role, I thought, *Well, maybe He's telling me to go dwell in that land!*

But as the days went by and I continued to seek His perfect way, He showed me through His Word and through wise counsel from those who highly regard His Word that the words I needed to say instead were, "Here am I, Lord. I'll stay!"

Don't get me wrong. I love where I am and what I'm doing, and I didn't seek an opportunity to leave. But when the opportunity was presented to me, I longed to "get chosen!" But in obedience to His perfect way, I had to make the difficult phone call to decline this particular opportunity.

God has been teaching me to live out the well-known phrase, "Wherever you are, be all there." So I will be "all in" right where I am— unless or until He chooses for me to serve Him somewhere else. That could be tomorrow. That could be next month. That could be next year. Or, it could be...never.

The bottom line is that when we honestly acknowledge that God's way is perfect, our hearts must truly, sincerely, and deeply be willing to go— or to stay.

This post first appeared on PetalsfromtheBasket.com on August 16, 2013.

IT'S TIME FOR A PRAISE WALK

If you're relatively new to this blog, you may be unfamiliar with a "Praise Walk." I first learned about this while visiting the Philippines in 1993. It was not original with my friends there; they had learned it many years before that from someone else. I won't take time to tell that story again, but I will summarize briefly what a "Praise Walk" is.

Start with *A* and think of a name, character quality, attribute, or action of God that starts with that letter. If you're doing this on a walk with a friend or in the car with your children, the next person will then do the same thing with *B*. Simply proceed through the alphabet. (You'll need to get a little creative with letters like *Q* and *X*.)

The fun thing is that you can even do this alone. Over the last twenty years since that walk in the Philippines, I have probably done hundreds of "Praise Walks, Sits, and Drives" by myself or with friends. To prepare my heart for worship on Sunday, I do this on my short two-mile drive to church, and I often find myself looking in the Bible for new names or attributes when I have my God-and-I-Time!

I encourage you to take a "Praise Walk" today—either by yourself or with a friend or family member(s). I spent some time last night having a "Praise Sit" in my favorite chair while listening to the rain. I was reminded again just how truly amazing God is! See if you can think of some new ones as you take your "Praise Walk" today!

This post first appeared on PetalsfromtheBasket.com on February 19, 2013.

CONSTRUCTION AHEAD

I was privileged to have lunch with an amazing local copywriter and author yesterday. We met at a delightful cafe and had such a wonderful time that I can hardly wait to spend time with her again! (And you can read her book: *Heaven without Her*, by Kitty Foth-Regner.)

As one who believes that arriving "on time" is actually arriving "late," I left home ridiculously early. I was later grateful for that cushion of time!

Because the route was very simple, I did not program the address into my Garmin (nicknamed "Greta"), but I simply jotted down on a scrap of paper the road names and the words "left" or "right" as mapped out for me the night before by MapQuest. I followed the route easily.

Then I saw it: "Road Closed Ahead." NOOOOOO! (And yes, I actually, honestly screamed!)

I've shared before that I am literally a gold medalist in being directionally challenged! I have *no* sense of direction—none!

So I followed the signs. However, after taking a winding road that didn't lead back to the original road, I was officially clueless as to my whereabouts—and I do mean clueless.

I pulled over, fretted, prayed (yes, in that order—shame on me!), finally programmed the address into my Garmin for Greta to find, and headed to the cafe without further delay!

Why didn't I do that in the first place?

Why don't I do that in my everyday life? So often I jot down the "basics" and think I've got it covered. But because I have no sense of direction within me apart from the leading of my Guide and Helper, I need His constant leading.

When I rely on Him I know I can confidently follow, and I'll end up in the right place! I don't have to wonder if the path is the right one. He created the path, so He will lead me every step along that path!

This morning my mom sent me the following awesome verses and the following reminder:

"As you have prayed, given your decision to the Lord, then made it, do not look back and wonder. Know it is the Lord's plan for you."

You are my hiding place; You preserve me from trouble; You surround me with songs of deliverance. Selah.

I will instruct you and teach you in the way which you should go; I will counsel you with My eye upon you.

Do not be as the horse or as the mule which have no understanding, whose trappings include bit and bridle to hold them in check, otherwise they will not come near to you.

Many are the sorrows of the wicked, but he who trusts in the Lord, loving-kindness shall surround him.

Be glad in the Lord and rejoice, you righteous ones; and shout for joy, all you who are upright in heart.

—Psalm 32:7–11, NASB

I might just need to nickname her Mama Greta!

_____

_____

_____

_____

_____

_____

_____

_____

_____

_____

_____

_____

This post first appeared on PetalsfromtheBasket.com on August 2, 2012.

LESSONS FROM THE HEART OF A CAREGIVER

I'm staring at this blank box on the screen into which I'm supposed to type inspirational, soul-stirring, life-changing words. I'm wondering how, when I feel so stripped of the ability to "have it all together," I'm supposed to create even a properly structured sentence. My very spirit feels empty, and my ability to cry out to those around me seems fruitless, since they are carrying the same burdens and also longing for the question marks to disappear and the exclamation points to return.

It's part of the ups and downs that come when a loved one is in hospice care. Uncertainty surrounds everything: Will my loved one still be here tomorrow? Will this forward progress continue for my loved one and give strength that we didn't think possible? How can I help my loved one maintain his joy when his daily routine allows for so little movement? What will happen…after? What should I be doing before…? How long will "before…" last? Was that a breath?

For those who may not know, my father began home hospice care on August 20, 2014. Right about that same time, my mom and I published our Bible study book, *But God*. So tonight, between the two previous paragraphs (when I was just pouring out my heart with no certainty where my writing would lead me) and the drying of my tears before starting this one, I decided to look through the book again—not as a coauthor but as a reader. As I mindlessly skimmed the pages, I kept simply repeating the title over and over in my mind: *But God…But God…But God.*

In a subtle demonstration of simply giving up, I closed the book and laid it on the floor next to my chair. It was then that the continuation of the title hit my heart—the heart of one who had actually coauthored the book to encourage other women—and I read the words "Question Mark or Exclamation Point?" In a case of tasting my own medicine, I was reminded that the difference comes in those two little words that wouldn't leave my mind: *But God.*

Yes, the question marks will remain regarding what happens next for my father, for my mother, for my family, for our friends, for me—for you. But in the midst of those uncertainties, one exclamatory element remains: But God!

"My flesh and my heart may fail, but God is the strength of my heart and my portion forever" (Psalm 73:26, NIV)!

_____

_____

_____

_____

_____

_____

_____

_____

This post first appeared on PetalsfromtheBasket.com on September 2, 2014.

REMEMBERING THE REASON FOR ALL WORSHIP MUSIC

I'm not on social media to argue or to complain. In fact, intentionally argumentative posts or comments seem to rarely change anyone's mind or belief system. Therefore, I choose to invest my time elsewhere.

My feed has contained many worship music-related posts lately. As I read some of the name-calling comments from the various views represented, my heart gets sad.

If you like more contemporary worship music, sing it, lead it, share it, respond to it for one reason only: to praise and give glory to God.

If you like more traditional worship music, sing it, lead it, share it, respond to it for one reason only: to praise and give glory to God.

Yes, it matters, as long as the goal matters. But I cannot and will not be the Holy Spirit in another person's life. Sing and worship with the purpose of giving glory to God—not for the purpose of proving to others that "your way" is "right." I've seen articles about how the traditionalists aren't singing anymore and also about how the contemporary music creates a style that no one but the worship team can follow. Broad paint brushes rarely get the details pictured accurately.

You have options. You hate the music? Go somewhere else to church, help to change it, or accept it. But arguing for the sole purpose of being right…isn't.

The "intolerance" of the perceived intolerance of others (by both "sides") is, quite honestly, becoming intolerable! What is the goal? From the heart…for His glory. Even on social media.

This post first appeared on PetalsfromtheBasket.com on May 28, 2014.

BUT I'M NOT A MOM

There is only one way for single women to view Mother's Day—the right way. There is no other option. So what is the right way?

Before I answer that question or write one more paragraph, I will include my standard disclaimer for a post like this. I'm a single woman, currently in my fifties, and I have never been married. The only thing that makes this "my choice" is that I choose, daily, to let God make those choices for me, and He has chosen for me to be without a spouse today. Since He knows best, I sincerely rejoice in His plan. Now—on with today's post!

On my sister Marcia's birthday, it would be foolish for me to be upset, stay home from her birthday celebration to watch a sad movie, and eat ginormous amounts of Hot Tamales (my comfort food of choice) just because the celebration isn't about me.

On my sister Karen's wedding anniversary, it would literally be obnoxious for me to write a blog post, asking the world to stop celebrating wedding anniversaries just because I don't have one to celebrate and telling them to be sensitive to my lack in their time of celebration.

Therefore, my fellow single women, this coming Sunday (Mother's Day), let's celebrate our own mothers as well as mothers everywhere for the amazing work that they do. Do you seriously think that when the pastor of the church has mothers stand up to recognize them for their all-too-often thankless role in shaping the generation of the future that your spiritual leader is, in actuality, saying, "What I really want you to do is turn around and take note of all the women not standing and inwardly laugh hysterically that there must be something horribly wrong with them since they are either childless or, worse yet, without a spouse altogether?"

As harsh as it may sound, get over yourself. This is not about you.

Too often, as singles, we turn situation after situation into what we think is a time of "permissible whining" because we are spouseless. Well, stop it! Right now! Because whining is not permissible, and it is not attractive!

We say that we trust God's leading, but then we fail to trust Him enough to obey His commands:

> "Do everything [yes, everything!] without grumbling...."
> —Philippians 2:14, NIV

> "Give thanks in all [yes, all] circumstances...."
> —I Thessalonians 5:18, NIV

> "Rejoice [yes, rejoice] with those who rejoice...."
> —Romans 12:15, NIV

WAIT! Don't say it yet! Because I know what some of you are thinking: "But, Brenda, the second half of that last verse you posted reminds believers to 'mourn with those who mourn.' So, I expect the street to go both ways!"

And you would be right. It should go both ways. But what if it doesn't? Does that excuse you from rejoicing on their behalf, particularly, in this setting, as they rejoice in the role of motherhood? You know the answer.

So, is it wrong to be sad that you are without a spouse or that you still don't have children after many years of trying and praying for a child? Of course not. Just remember to keep it a desire and not a demand!

And more importantly, remember to rejoice with those who have been given what you long for. Focus on others this weekend. Applaud those amazing females when they stand in church during their far-too-brief moment of recognition!

Look beyond your own garden and see the beautiful array of flowers that we all get the opportunity to celebrate this weekend!

I'm throwing in this extra story, even though it might seem to slightly contradict all of the above…well…because I can! My niece Jillian calls me or texts me every year on Mother's Day and thanks me for being "a woman of influence" in her life, knowing that my desire for motherhood is not one that will likely ever be fulfilled at this point and choosing to lift me up on a day when the evil ick whispers in my ear more often than he should be allowed to do!

So let me encourage you—both married women and single women—to think of a single woman you could encourage this weekend by thanking her for her influence in your life.

No, you're not trying to make it a "substitute Mother's Day" celebration for her—she's not a mom. You are simply using this widely celebrated weekend that honors mothers as an impetus to celebrate women who have impacted your life! (In the process, it just might help to remind you that you're not the only one who is not a mom.)

The bottom line? To my friends and family who are moms, I wish you the most joyful of all Mother's Days!

To my friends who, like myself, are not moms, I wish you a day of joy as you look outward and celebrate those who are!

This post first appeared on PetalsfromtheBasket.com on May 9, 2014.

WHERE'S MY SHOVEL

It snowed most of the day in my area of Wisconsin on Thursday. From the sounds of it, my friends and family in the Northeast are going to spend much of today and tomorrow getting what we got—and much, much more. So as I sat down to write, I had snow on my mind. Maybe that's why I thought about this verse:

> "Purify me from my sins, and I will be clean; wash me, and I will be whiter than snow." —Psalm 51:7, NLT

As it snowed, I watched the snowplows go back and forth at frequent intervals, keeping the roads cleared and safe for travel. They didn't wait until the end of the snowfall—late at night. No, those hard-working crews know the basic principle that if you let the snow pile up, it gets packed down, and/or it becomes too difficult to move because of how much has accumulated.

My parents also apply that concept with their driveway. Though their association has a plowing service that comes after a certain number of inches of snowfall, my parents and their sweet next-door neighbors will often have two of the driest, ice-free driveways in the neighborhood. Why? Because they have gone out frequently and not only shoveled the main path; they have also cleared away those areas in the corners that are hard for the plows to reach.

A neighbor in Michigan, Jeff, would often tease me about shoveling after only three inches of snow had fallen. "Hey, Brenda—you know we're still gonna get five more inches, don't you?" I would reply that it was much easier for me to do three inches, and then two inches, and then another three inches than it was to attempt to shovel through eight inches of snow at the end of the storm!

This same "shoveling principle" is true in my spiritual life. I see this in three ways, as represented by the three true scenarios above:

(1) If I "plow away" the sin before it has a chance to accumulate, the path is clear for God to accomplish His work in me.

(2) If I frequently take care of the hidden areas of my heart where sin can pile up—even though they're out of plain sight—my life can shine for Christ in a dark world.

(3) If I follow David's example in Psalm 51 and ask God daily to cleanse and purify my heart (whiter than snow!), it makes sense that there won't be an opportunity for the sin to enlarge in its impact and its scope.

Just like plowing away the snow, keeping a "short sin account" keeps the path to victory clear!

Suggested reading: Psalm 51

This post first appeared on PetalsfromtheBasket.com on February 8, 2013.

SHE'S ONE OF OURS

With the Olympics just around the corner, much is being said about the athletes who are in their final stages of preparation. As I watched a news clip about one team of athletes, the focus was on how this particular group had recently given interviews that were a poor reflection on their status as Olympians. The reporter concluded his piece by stating that these athletes needed to remember that their actions both on and off the field are done as representatives of the United States. He added that we need to be proud to say of each of them, "She's one of ours!"

For some reason, that hit me between the eyes. As a believer, my actions— "on and off the field"— are to bring honor to the One I represent—the Lord Jesus Christ. The particular athletes that were on the screen had used humanly understandable excuses for their behavior, but the news reporter kept coming back to the bottom line that they represent the United States at all times because they are known as US Olympians. Period.

Paul gave Timothy wise advice regarding this that we should all follow, regardless of our age:

> "Let no one look down on your youthfulness, but rather in speech, conduct, love, faith and purity, show yourself an example of those who believe" (I Timothy 4:12, NASB).

Today's post is a short one because its lesson in my life was simple: I am to live every area of my life in a way that positively represents the One Whose name I carry. Period.

This post first appeared on PetalsfromtheBasket.com on July 25, 2012.

LESSONS FROM NINEVAH

Jonah and the great fish (usually called "whale") is a Bible story most people have heard at some point in their lives. There are numerous songs about this story that help children learn early in their lives that instant obedience goes hand in hand with a joyful heart. It's such an important true story that it has its own book in the Bible.

The pastor's sermon last week was on the book of Jonah, and the lessons I learned have been on the forefront of my mind since Sunday. Continuing with the patriotic theme, I couldn't help but think of Ninevah as I have prayed this week for God to bless America.

I won't take your time to recount the entire story of Jonah's assignment from God. I will, however, encourage you to take less than ten minutes to read the entire book of Jonah in the Bible. Seriously—less than ten minutes! The city of Ninevah was so morally corrupt that God assigned Jonah the task of telling them that destruction was coming. (Jonah 1:1–2, NIV: "The word of the Lord came to Jonah son of Amittai: 'Go to the great city of Nineveh and preach against it, because its wickedness has come up before me.'")

Now begins the most familiar part of the story. Jonah goes the opposite direction from Ninevah, earning him a God-ordained "time out" in the disgusting belly of a huge fish. After three days and a lesson learned,

Jonah received a command from God a second time (Jonah 3:1) to go to Ninevah. This time, Jonah obeyed and proclaimed the message that God was going to destroy Ninevah.

Here comes the lesson that we as Americans can learn from this sinful city: the people of Ninevah realized the power of God and chose to turn from their sins and to acknowledge Him as the One True God! As a result, we read these words in Jonah 3:10: "When God saw what they did and how they turned from their evil ways, he relented and did not bring on them the destruction he had threatened" (NIV). Their sincerity touched the heart of God!

During this week of praying for America, I have found myself thinking, "Yeah, right. This nation will *never* fully turn back to God. But I'll pray anyway." Then I thought of Ninevah. My faith should not be in believing that the people of America will turn to God, but my faith should be in the God Who is waiting with open arms to "forgive their sin and heal their land" (II Chronicles 7:14, NIV). Oh, that our repentant hearts would touch the heart of God!

Lord, today I pray that You will open the eyes and hearts of Americans as a nation. Thank You for the mercy and grace You give to us as individuals. It is that same mercy and grace that I pray You will show to our country today. May Your name be glorified in America—and in my life. Thank You for what You will do, Father! Amen.

This post first appeared on PetalsfromtheBasket.com on July 5, 2012.

MINGLING WITH SPARROWS

Did you ever watch *That Girl* on television, either when it originally aired or via one of the oldies channels?

In one of my favorite episodes, "Ann Marie," played by Marlo Thomas, goes to an elegant business event with long-time boyfriend, "Donald Hollinger," played by Ted Bessell. In this episode, Ann was hesitant to attend the event, not knowing anyone there and feeling uncertain what to talk about with the other guests.

Upon arriving, Donald encouraged her to "go mingle." Ann quickly realized that the noise level of the event prohibited people from carrying on meaningful conversations. In her humorous yet gracious way, Ann walked up to various groups and used conversational tones while saying, "Here a mingle (nods at one guest), there a mingle (nods at another guest, then takes in the entire group as she ends with), everywhere a mingle-mingle." Not really listening or not being able to hear, they would nod in reply, as though she had said something brilliant. She would then head off and repeat the process with another group.

The above scene from *That Girl* often comes to mind when I enter a "church-wide fellowship." As a woman at church without a spouse, I often have the same hesitancy about entering a room where I know few if any people! But I know that fellowship with other believers is important, and so I go. I "mingle." I leave early.

Yesterday my new church had its annual community-wide outreach—a patriotic service sharing the Gospel, honoring Veterans, and culminating in a ginormous picnic, car show, and play area with huge inflatables for the kids. I desperately wanted to attend this event after the morning service, but I did not want to go alone. "Here a mingle, there a mingle" is just a little out of place in a picnic atmosphere!

A lady from my Bible study, Pat, told me last week that she would also be at the middle service of the three services offered. However, I neglected to ask her at that time if I could join her for the picnic.

As I exited the auditorium and entered the large foyer, I sincerely prayed silently in my heart, becoming totally oblivious to anything or anyone, "Lord, you know I desire to enjoy the fellowship and fun of this picnic. There are thousands of people here, but please help me find Pat. Thank You, Lord." I slowly blinked as if in a silent "Amen." As I mentally reentered the world around me, and just as my blink ended, Pat walked right in front of me!

I instantly thought of Matthew 10:29–31 (NLT):

> "What is the price of two sparrows—one copper coin? But not a single sparrow can fall to the ground without your Father knowing it. And the very hairs on your head are all numbered. So don't be afraid; you are more valuable to God than a whole flock of sparrows."

These verses reminded me that my loving God cares about every need that I have. I cannot escape His care! If He knows what's going on in the life of a little sparrow (and He does) and if He can help me find a new acquaintance in a vast crowd of people (and He can—and did), then He can care for every need I face in this week!

By the way, yes, I enjoyed the picnic! So I'll leave the "mingling" to the flock of sparrows. I have friendships to form and fellowships to attend!

This post first appeared on PetalsfromtheBasket.com on June 25, 2012.

THE DANGER OF THE BACKWARD GLANCE

When my nephew was about ten years old, he was running backward (for a school activity), fell, and severely broke his wrist. He's now headed to med school—so that tells you the time span for this—but through the years, I have been reminded often of this event and have thought about the foolishness of running backward when we are meant to move forward.

Yes, it's true that we look to the past for lessons (both painful and joyful), for experiences, and for the people and friendships that walked through them with us. But do an experiment for me, will you? Stop right now and turn your head as far as you can to look behind you. In fact, after making sure you have a clear path in front of you, try to walk forward while looking backward. When you're done, come pick back up at the next paragraph. No hurry…I'll wait!

Unless you're a uniquely gifted contortionist, you probably found the same two things to be true that I did:

The view is partially obstructed when you try to look backward.

No matter how hard you try, you don't get the big picture when you're attempting to turn your neck as far to one side as you can. When I spend my days looking at how things were, at how they should have been, or at what happened in the past—even when I think that what happened was great—I tend to lose the big picture. I see only the elements I want to see or need to see. My futile attempts to gaze upon what I long to hold onto—whether joy or bitterness, anger or delight—are only partial in their perspective.

I neglect to see that on the other side of that element is the hand of God, lovingly orchestrating the events or the individuals in such a way that my life would benefit, in that given moment, from their influence and for the purpose of propelling me forward. But when my focus is skewed by emotions or unmet expectations, causing me to glance backward with a longing that is no longer a part of the plan for my present, I am missing out on the delight of what that moment, event, or individual did to help guide me into the present moment.

Hebrews 12:2 reminds us to look *to* Jesus—not to look *back* at Jesus! He is in front of me, leading the way, with the entire big picture in view! That results in a trust that longs to keep a forward look!

It's difficult to move forward when you're looking backward.

In fact, when you're worried about stumbling over what's in front of you, it can consume your thoughts, preventing you from moving either forward or backward. You just stand there, paralyzed—afraid to take the next step, because your glance is backward, but your body is headed forward. It's awkward. It's frightening. And…it's unnecessary. Turn your head—your mind, your heart, your focus—and take a good look at where you are and where you want to go. Then keep looking at that goal—and go there!

In the Bible, the author Paul, who had a past that was as sordid and bitterness-inducing as they come, wrote these words in Philippians 3:13–14 (NLT): "No, dear brothers and sisters, I have not achieved it, but I focus on this one thing: forgetting the past and looking forward to what lies ahead, I press on to reach the end of the race and receive the heavenly prize for which God, through Christ Jesus, is calling us."

So learn from the past, embrace the events and individuals from the past who have influenced and made an impact on your present, and then keep a forward focus, eyes fixed on Jesus, pressing toward the goal of being what He wants you to be and doing what He wants you to do today, walking with joyful anticipation down whatever path He has planned for your future!

This post first appeared on PetalsfromtheBasket.com on January 11, 2014.

THE RIDE OF A LIFETIME!

School is already back in session in some areas. *What?* Isn't it somewhere around June 1, and summer is just beginning? Then again, the extremely hot season most of us in the States have experienced won't allow us to deny that summer has been in full swing for several months!

If I were to write the traditional "what-I-did-on-my-summer-vacation" paper often assigned early in the school year, it would look something like this:

What I Did on My Summer Vacation
by Brenda Strohbehn

This summer I rode the biggest roller coaster of my life! It was huge! It went way up and then way down—and then it went back up again! There were twists and turns that made me wish I could jump off the "ride" right in the middle of it. There were people waiting in line and people standing around, observing the ride who shouted, "Jump off the ride now! The next turn is too scary!"

And it was scary. So I hung on tighter. I was supposed to be on that ride, and if I were try to leave in the middle of it, pain and injury would be a certainty. Sometimes staying in the ride is actually safer than trying to run away from it!

But they kept shouting their warnings and their thoughts regarding how silly it was for me to be on this crazy ride. Some of them spoke softly and even took the time to whisper with kindness: "You would really do much better on another ride; a softer, more certain ride is the one you need to be on."

Others were quite blunt in their opinions of the ride I was on: "What are you—*crazy*? That's not the ride for you. I've been on other rides that are better. Now stop being stubborn and get down from there right this minute! You're going to fall out or get injured sitting up there all by yourself going up and down and all around. I mean it. Don't make me tell you again!"

But what they couldn't see from the angle at which they were watching the ride was that I was not alone. In the seats all around me were my family members and some very dear friends who were there to keep me from jumping out, to prevent me from falling out, to keep me from giving up and to offer words of love and encouragement around every turn!

They reminded me often throughout the ride that the One Who had orchestrated my getting on this ride was also aware of what was at the top of each peak and at the bottom of each "drop." They pointed me to the written words that guaranteed that He knew what was around every turn, and He was watching out for me by guiding me through them!

Those were the voices I chose to listen to. Those were the ones I gathered around me as I entered the ride, knowing that they would do exactly what they did—encourage me!

So in spite of its uncertainties, stomach-dropping moments, and conflicting crowd noises, I'm grateful that I spent my summer "vacation" on the craziest roller coaster ride of my lifetime!

The God Who spoke these words many years ago to His chosen people is the same One Who provides His care for me today: "For I know the plans I have for you," says the Lord. "They are plans for good and not for disaster, to give you a future and a hope."

— Jeremiah 29:11, NLT

This post first appeared on PetalsfromtheBasket.com on August 14, 2012.

DOES WHAT I DO REALLY MATTER?

Sitting at the big round table at Cracker Barrel today, I had a breakthrough moment where something I've been struggling with suddenly vanished into insignificance. (I also had a ginormous serving of food that probably could have and should have fed an entire third-world country, but that's a whole 'nother story!)

I'm sharing this struggle because I'm certain that I can't be the only one.

I want to matter. I don't give a frip about money or position or recognition or accumulated hoo-ha. I simply want to matter. For many years I have said that "when my time comes," I want a simple grave marker the size of a 4 x 6 card for a tombstone, but I want it to say my name, my dates of birth and death, and then, in order to show that what I did mattered and mattered for the right reasons, I want the words of John 17:4 included: "I have brought You glory on earth by finishing the work You gave me to do" (NIV).

Yet lately, from the confines of a three-story home filled with beautiful globally acquired treasures and people that I love, I've realized that…I pretty much don't matter. Now before you send me counseling materials and dial the help-a-friend hotline for advice, let me explain.

In my current situation, serving as a caregiver for my aging parents in their home, it's hard to believe that crushing pills, applying lotions, providing physical support for someone else's frail and weakened body, turning the TV on precisely one minute before the evening news, reading a one-page devotional each evening, or helping with numerous other seemingly menial tasks actually matters anywhere outside these walls. And yet, I realize that it doesn't have to. It has to matter to my parents and to God. And I believe that it does.

But I shamefacedly and openly confess that this leaves me feeling lonely, insignificant in the big picture, and wondering if I'll ever really "matter" beyond this street address.

And then, in a God-directed moment, a former student/now friend who once worked in my office at a small college in the north woods of Wisconsin and now serves as a missionary in Puerto Rico with her dear family sent me a message the other day to see how far my "new" town was from the toll road. To make a long story, well, not as long, I'll just say that I ended up getting to meet my friends at Cracker Barrel for lunch today. I had never met their three awesome kids, so that was an "Auntie Brenda" blessing just thrown in as a bonus!

As I talked with the husband about some editing work my freelance business has done and will be doing for him, it hit me: You, Brenda Strohbehn, get to have a part in something that matters. From inside the walls of your home, your work, your words, your life get to intertwine with unknown numbers of people as you pray for, edit, and encourage the publication of this printed material—material that matters.

And that matters.

Moms with little kids at home and whose days are spent "confined" by going only the distance between the kitchen, the bathroom, and the living room certainly feel this way at times. But don't you see, my amazing faith-friends? That matters! The work you do there matters in perhaps a globally impacting way down the road as your child travels for business when he or she becomes an adult and shares the wonderful truths that you taught him or her in that confined space at a time when you thought you didn't matter. It matters when your child, as my friends now are doing, becomes vocationally committed to sharing the Good News with others in lands that God says matter.

Every person, doing the work that he or she is called to do, matters. What you're doing today? It matters. Because what Christ did matters, doing the work He has given you to do in this moment matters.

The only time it can't matter is when you're unfocused and distracted into thinking that it doesn't matter.

This post first appeared on PetalsfromtheBasket.com on October 17, 2014.

HOW'D YOU GET SO SMART?

This past week, I turned fifty-three years old. I don't know why, but that somehow seems monumentally older than fifty-two, and I'm living with this sense that I should now have the ability to pour forth words of wisdom and live the serene life of someone who's got it all together. You know me—I'm doing neither.

In fact, the older I get, the more I realize that gaining wisdom is an ongoing process; it's not a one-time event or something acquired automatically at a given age. As for that serene life, I'm not so sure I even want that. After all, pain and conflict have a way of letting us know that we're not numb, and that we are still very much alive.

However, I confess that I do want to be wise. The book of Proverbs in the Bible has much to say about wisdom, and it strongly emphasizes that getting wisdom is a good thing. So I've chosen four areas in which I want to demonstrate wisdom in the year ahead.

Spiritual wisdom:

You'd expect that from a faith-based blog writer, wouldn't you? But it's true. I want to be wise in where I place my trust and in how I worship my God. I want to demonstrate wisdom in how I learn about Him through church services and Bible studies. And I want to be wise by being deliberate about spending personal "God-and-I-time" with Him each day—sitting at His feet, as it were, and "listening" to the words He speaks to me from the pages of the Bible. When His wisdom finds its way into my heart, I will think wisely, live in a wise way, and speak words of wisdom.

Relational wisdom:

I'm a planner. I like to know what will happen. God knows the outcome already, so I just don't have a clue why I get so riled up about my various relationships. I really want to have wisdom in this area, so again, I will need to be deliberate in keeping my first and most important relationship—my relationship with God—as my primary focus. That allows me to contentedly leave all other relationships under His control!

Financial wisdom:

This has been a weak area for me. I made a lot of poor choices in my twenties and thirties—You mean, money *doesn't* grow on trees?—and it was an endless cycle of attempting to repair not only my habits but the ensuing damage. However, by God's almighty grace, I now live with the knowledge that stuff is just stuff—it has lost its once-powerful allure, and it no longer enslaves me! But that freedom is based on daily, minute-by-minute choices to be a wise steward with what He entrusts to me. By the way, this includes implementing wisdom in how I use the skills—both business skills and personal talents—that I have been given. Who cares if I die wealthy? No one. Who cares if I made a difference through wise use of my funds, talents, and resources? Those whose lives were impacted by their wise use.

Physical wisdom:

I can't even believe I'm confessing this on a public blog, but…here goes. I'm currently a lousy representation of physical wisdom. Lousy—times seven! Though my explanations of the weight I've gained in recent years are solid (erratic eating habits, sitting at a computer for the majority of the day, age, post-surgery body, blah-blah-blah…), the excuses are weak. They clearly portray my unwise choices in what I eat, when I eat it, and how I eat it. So, in the year ahead—and for many years to come, God willing—I'm deliberately choosing wisely, exercising, and remembering that I need to be and feel my best so that nothing—especially not embarrassment about "letting myself go"—distracts me from being wise in all the other areas.

So at the end of my life, when someone asks—and I hope they'll be able to ask this—"How'd you get so smart?" I hope I'll be able to say that, in 2014, I utilized God-given wisdom by making God-honoring choices.

This post first appeared on PetalsfromtheBasket.com on January 11, 2014.

MY FRIEND ANNIE

The other day, I posted the lyrics of an old song, "He Giveth More Grace." Though I sang it throughout the morning, I wanted to make sure I had the words right before adding it on my blog post. The site where I found the lyrics also contained a story about their author, Annie Johnson Flint, and I was drawn into reading it.

I have a new "friend" as a result. No, I never met her. No, I had never heard of her before that time. Yes, she is deceased. But still, I now count her as a friend. She impacted my life and pointed it heavenward as her words crossed my path. I won't tell the entire story, but here is the extremely abbreviated version:

Born in 1866, Annie was the first child born to Eldon and Jean Johnson. Only three years after Annie's birth, her mother died during the delivery of Annie's younger sister. Knowing that he could not properly care for the little girls, Eldon took them to the home of a widow of a Civil War soldier. They were only in that home for two years.

The widow's neighbors, Mr. and Mrs. Flint, took the two Johnson girls into their home at that time and not only loved them and gave them their name, but they introduced them to Christ! Annie grew in her love for the things of the Lord and in her love of poetry. Her optimistic nature was clearly seen in her writings.

Skip ahead to her post high school years. Annie found out as a very young woman (barely out of high school) that she had arthritis. It was extreme and debilitating and rendered her as a crippled invalid in very little time. Her resources were minimal, but God allowed her to use the skills He had given her to begin creating greeting cards—not for her own sake but to be an encouragement to others.

Her journals contain very little regarding the pains and sorrows caused by her illness, but they tell of what God allowed her to do for others and how He provided for her every need! She took the comfort she received from the Lord and used it to be a comfort to those around her—and beyond, to 2012! [II Corinthians 1:3–4!]

> [She] always stated that her poems were born of the need of others and not from her own need; but one knows full well that she never could have written as she did for the comfort and help of thousands of others if she had not had the background of facing those very crises in her own life.

I am personally thankful for this dear servant of God whose life has left its imprint on my heart.

Her life was lived, as someone has said, from hand to mouth, but as she liked to have it expressed, the mouth was hers, and the hand was God's, and His hand was never empty.

Information collected from
http://www.preceptaustin.org/annie_johnson_flint's_biography.htm

This post first appeared on PetalsfromtheBasket.com on May 12, 2012.

GRAY AND GRATEFUL

During my "growing-up years," our family verse was Matthew 6:33, "But seek ye first the kingdom of God, and his righteousness; and all these things shall be added unto you" (KJV). This is an awesome verse at the conclusion of a passage reminding us that we don't need to worry about what we will wear, what we will eat, or what we will drink! We are commanded, yes commanded, to seek His kingdom above everything else, and all these things *will* be provided by Him!

At the time of my parents' fiftieth wedding anniversary (ten years ago!), they added the following verse to their "family verses" for the "second half" of their journey together:

> "Now that I am old and gray, do not abandon me, O God. Let me proclaim Your power to this new generation, Your mighty miracles to all who come after me." – Psalm 71:18, NLT

I recently heard them recite this together after their morning Bible reading, and soon after that, I found myself without employment and its related evening activities—additional time that needed to be used wisely. It was the memory of hearing this verse that prompted the recent publication of a few e-books—with more to come!

My parents are now in their eighties. (Lest you think I'm being a horrid daughter by sharing their ages, they are quite fine with it: they've worked hard and earned every gray hair they have—many of which I'm sure came from me!) Though they used to travel and speak in churches around the country and around the world—primarily through the ministry of family conferences and also while representing a Christian camp—they are not able to travel much anymore. However, they continue to desire first and foremost to continue to have a ministry to others, sharing Who God is, the salvation from sin that He provides, and what He is continuing to teach them as they learn more of Him.

Enter: Psalm 71:18.

Change, just for the sake of change or just for the sake of not doing it "the old way," seems to me to be just a lot of work and a spinning of the wheels without forward momentum. However, change that utilizes new methods that are now available or that is being done for the sake of greater outreach—without changing the foundational message—is wise and allows us to move forward!

This "new generation" (as the NLT calls them in Psalm 71:18) is a technologically savvy generation. Therefore, we who are becoming or are already "old and gray" need to recognize that we may need to make some changes in order to reach them with the Gospel of Christ, always remembering that the Good News itself never changes!

Therefore, I view books, e-books, websites, and blogs as ways to allow ministry to others to continue, even if the authors can't share the information face-to-face at this time. It is a way to reach "this new generation" as well as "all who come after me!"

_____

_____

_____

_____

This post first appeared on PetalsfromtheBasket.com on April 25, 2012.

KEEP LOOKING UP!

Sometime between 8:30 and 9:30 p.m. each evening, my mom and I help my dad sit on the edge of his bed for a few minutes. After raising the top of the hospital bed in his bedroom, I generally lean in and wrap my arms around his entire torso, and he wraps his arms around me as I push my right knee solidly into the side of the mattress so that we can use our combined strength to swing his body from facing forward on the bed to facing the side wall in their bedroom. While we are accomplishing this easier-than-it-sounds task, my mom is swinging his legs from the top of the bed downward to a ninety-degree angle so that his feet reach the floor in order to create the "seated" position for him. Again, no small task, but it only takes seconds.

Once Dad is in the seated position on the edge of the bed, it's clear that he's unsteady on his own. We support him with our strength, and then we encourage him to "look up." This gives him a stable focal point and helps to steady him. When he looks up, you can literally see the relaxation and calm that replaces the uncertainty caused by the frailty of his Parkinson's-affected body.

After a few minutes of chitchat and a few oft-repeated memories about the days when we took the family pictures that grace the wall he is facing, it's time to help him stand by the bed. With Mom on one side of him, circling her left arm so that the bend in her elbow fits tightly under his right armpit and I on the opposite side using my right arm to accomplish the same position with his left side, we generally recite the same three reminders:

1. Make sure your feet are firmly planted.

2. Let us help you.

3. Look up. (Again, this creates a solid focal point, providing the ability to stand firmly without wobbling.)

Tonight, however, I realized that once he's up and doing well, his glance generally goes back down to the floor, and invariably one of us will say what is quickly becoming the fourth reminder:

4. Keep looking up.

If you've read this blog for any period of time at all, you know right where this is headed because my physically frail, spiritually faithful father taught us all a huge lesson with his life tonight. So here's a quick application for our own lives:

1. Make sure your feet are firmly planted.

The unchanging Word of God should provide the foundation for every choice, every decision, every business move, every relationship, every thought, every word, every action—everything! Read it. Know it. Apply it. Opinions and emotions come and go. God's Word never, ever, ever changes! Seeking wisdom in its pages should be the first go-to in our attempts to take the next steps. (Read James 1:5.)

2. Let us help you.

You weren't meant to live life on your own. Others are in your life to encourage you, teach you, help you, support you, pray for you, love you, and so much more. And they are also there so that you can reach out and do the same for them! There is strength in numbers—utilize it! (Read Galatians 6:2.)

3. Look up.

Look to the unwavering goodness of Jesus. Don't be distracted by extraneous attractions or things that this temporal world tells you matter. Fix your eyes on His amazing, solid, always-the-same grace! (Read Hebrews 12:2.)

4. Keep looking up!

It's so easy to get "comfortable" and let our upward gaze slowly find its way back down to the horizontal trivialities that so easily distract us from our "sanctified stare!" Don't stop. It takes effort. It's a deliberate choice. It's got to be intentional. It needs to be continuous. Choose. Decide. Determine not to let anything be so important to you that it takes your eyes off of Jesus for even one fleeting moment. Choose Christ. Then keep choosing Christ. (Read II Timothy 3:14.)

To know the power of a stance grounded on an immovable foundation, supported by other believers whose desire is to see you standing strong, look to Jesus. Look up. But don't stop there.

Keep looking up!

Thanks for the lesson, Dad.

_____

_____

_____

_____

_____

This post first appeared on PetalsfromtheBasket.com on September 10, 2014.

OF SHADOWS AND SPOTLIGHTS

"Place your focus on Christ."

"Place your faith in Christ."

"Place your future in Christ."

Those words have come out of my mouth many times as I have taught small groups of ladies or as I have spoken to larger audiences at retreats or women's conferences. So please understand the embarrassment on my face and in my heart as I share this next thought:

It's actually quite easy to "point the spotlight on Christ" when the spotlight is on me.

But what happens when the spotlight is removed—when I find myself to be an "unknown" in a new crowd of faces? Suddenly, it's now actually quite easy to turn the spotlight back on myself and all the changes that I somehow think are oh, so traumatic, apparently seeking some sort of validation from my new surroundings. (Insert a pathetic-sounding round of "Oh, poor me; no one here knows me, and I'm feeling so alone," and you'll have the tone of this pity party.)

But I won't dwell there long. In fact, I'm going to close this post with exactly what I recorded in my journal—preceded by a bunch of selfishly personal thoughts that I'm not about to post here—after being struck by the amazing thing I saw when reading John chapter three today:

"Once again the humility of John the Baptist comes to the forefront, and he steps into the shadows to shine a spotlight on Christ: 'He must increase, but I must decrease.'"

Lord, thank You for removing me from the comfort of the oh, so small and temporary spotlight and placing me in the shadows, for there, I can see the importance of the spotlight that I am able to shine on You—and You alone—when it is unhindered by anything else, free to illuminate Your face, Your heart, and Your love.

This post first appeared on PetalsfromtheBasket.com on April 3, 2014.

GRACE—JUST GRACE

We sing "Amazing Grace," but do we really believe that it's amazing?

A former neighbor had an affair with a married man, resulting in a child that she chose to keep. (He's an adorable little three-year-old boy with a personality that won't quit!) But his mother truly believes that she deserves nothing better than casual flings because she "ruined" her life. She believes that no man who is "worth anything" would want her.

A childhood friend went through a painful divorce many years ago now and actually thinks that God can't use him because of it. So now he lives without true hope, thinking that God somehow loves him in a lesser way. Because of that way of thinking, he lives a life that is based on temporal values and temporal relationships. He thinks he deserves nothing deeper than that.

A high school student was known as—and labeled as—a "goof off" during his junior high years, primarily due to a major change in location for his family, which he was struggling through. Though the behavior was no longer a part of his life, he just "gave up" on school, on his dreams, and on believing that he could make positive changes in his life.

Grace isn't grace because we earn it, deserve it, or have any rights to it. That's what makes it grace. When we realize the true potency of grace, we move beyond the past and claim "strength for today and bright hope for tomorrow."

Through grace, we make change. By accepting the reality and power of grace, we can accept God's unconditional love. By grace, we live transformed lives.

Regardless of the lack of grace bestowed upon us by others whose pride says, "Thank goodness, that's not me! I never would have made those wrong choices," we have the unfathomable grace of God that says, "I valued you enough to offer you My grace. Therefore, My grace gives you value. Accept it and live accordingly."

When we try to add our worth to that, we can't claim what He offers. We'll come up short, and we'll think we only deserve to continue on the downward path that we're currently on.

But because of grace—just His amazing grace—we have hope. We can change. We can move forward. We can realize that His grace is more than enough. We can sing, with renewed hearts, "Through many dangers, toils, and snares, I have already come. 'Tis grace hath brought me safe thus far, and grace will lead me home."

This post first appeared on PetalsfromtheBasket.com on March 15, 2014.

EIGHT SIMPLE WORDS

Watching football; getting a manicure. Attending formal black tie dinners; sitting on the floor with my back propped against the couch while eating pizza. Gleaning wisdom from the older generation; gleaning wisdom from the younger generation. Talking to friends; listening to strangers (and accepting them as friends). Elegant order and design; eclectic, sentimental spontaneity—just because. Accepting items; living experiences. Modern colors; weathered antiques. Speaking to crowds; giggling with children.

These are a few of my favorite things.

While it might sound carefree and free-spirited to have a life that is literally a study in contrasts, it always bothered me that my interests were so vast and varied. I wanted to be one of those people who had a specific style, a talent at which I excelled, a home that I lived in for more than ten years, a "thing" for which I was well-known.

Then I realized that God gave me broad interests, skills at which I was good (not great), experiences in many different small towns and large cities, and friends and acquaintances that encompass all of them. Without those interests, skills, and experiences, my world would be so small, because I wouldn't have met and interacted with so many amazing, everyday, spectacular leaders and followers in my lifetime—so far!

Occasionally, I try to make it a point to take time to tell my friends and associates how blessed I am to know them and to share my gratitude for their impact on my life.

Yet, as one who is sincere and generous with her gratitude and praise, I confess that sometimes it's nice to hear that in return. (I've never done the "love language" thing that some of my friends are talking about, but I think that's mine—if that even is one; if not, they should add it!) But it can't be mustered up. The spoken word has to be genuine to matter. And today, I received exactly that. But it wasn't in the form that you might think. It was in eight amazing words that reminded me that there is a *constant* in the midst of everything else that is changing:

> "He will neither fail you nor abandon you."
> —Deuteronomy 31:6, 8, NLT

He made me. He knows me. He cares. He gets it. He's invested in me. He won't fail me. He won't abandon me. He loves me unconditionally. He's the constant in a life filled with contrasts and changes.

And suddenly, these unchanging truths became my new favorite things.

This post first appeared on PetalsfromtheBasket.com on January 16, 2014.

LALALALALA—I CAN'T HEEEEAR YOU!

They're called "spoiler alerts." Do you know what I mean? It's when, let's say, you're attending a birthday party for your grandma, so you miss your favorite Olympic event, but you set your TV to record the competition so that you can watch it later. You return home just in time for the evening news, and they announce, "Spoiler alert! If you don't want to know the results of today's Olympic events, put your TV on mute in three seconds. Three…two…." And you mute your TV or put your fingers in your ears, while loudly and melodically saying, "Lalalalala—I can't heeeear you" in order not to hear what you really *want* to know.

But sometimes we also use this technique to drown out what we *should* hear but *don't* want to know! On Wednesday, I was to read Psalm 51 as part of the daily Bible reading that I'm doing this month. But I found that I as I looked at my reading list (i.e., read the spoiler alert—the fact that I knew what the chapter contained) and because I did not want to have those words prick my needy heart, I closed my spiritual ears and lyrically, though nonverbally, demonstrated a spirit of, "Lalalalala—I can't heeeear you." I became obsessed with color coding the chapter, looking for "key words," and methodically performing my otherwise well-motivated Bible study habits in order to drown out the words I needed to "hear" by just reading them.

Yet, in His mercy, the Lord patiently spoke, as I sat there with open-palm-covered ears. And as His words began to reach their target audience—the depths of my heart—I lowered my hands and clasped them together in a prayer of repentance for my unwillingness to simply listen to my Master's instructions.

Then, with my heart and my ears open to His tender voice, I tearfully read the precious words of Psalm 51. I'll close with some of those today, praying that you will not be found with your hands over your ears as you read.

Spoiler alert: it will reach your heart if you let it!

1 Have mercy on me, O God,
according to your unfailing love;
according to your great compassion
blot out my transgressions.
2 Wash away all my iniquity
and cleanse me from my sin.

3 For I know my transgressions,
and my sin is always before me.
4 Against you, you only, have I sinned
and done what is evil in your sight;
so you are right in your verdict
and justified when you judge.
5 Surely I was sinful at birth,
sinful from the time my mother conceived me.
6 Yet you desired faithfulness even in the womb;
you taught me wisdom in that secret place.

7 Cleanse me with hyssop, and I will be clean;
wash me, and I will be whiter than snow.
8 Let me hear joy and gladness;
let the bones you have crushed rejoice.
9 Hide your face from my sins
and blot out all my iniquity.

10 Create in me a pure heart, O God,
and renew a steadfast spirit within me.
11 Do not cast me from your presence
or take your Holy Spirit from me.
12 Restore to me the joy of your salvation
and grant me a willing spirit, to sustain me.

13 Then I will teach transgressors your ways,
so that sinners will turn back to you.
14 Deliver me from the guilt of bloodshed, O God,
you who are God my Savior,
and my tongue will sing of your righteousness.
15 Open my lips, Lord,
and my mouth will declare your praise.
16 You do not delight in sacrifice, or I would bring it;
you do not take pleasure in burnt offerings.
17 My sacrifice, O God, is a broken spirit;
a broken and contrite heart
you, God, will not despise.

—Psalm 51:1–17, NIV

This post first appeared on PetalsfromtheBasket.com on August 23, 2013.

SHH…

"Be still, and know that I am God…." (Psalm 46:10, NIV)

Life lesson #427:

I've been looking at the blank computer screen for almost thirty minutes. Yet, I still can't think of one intelligent thing to say or even one topic to write about today. But I still learned something in those thirty minutes:

Sometimes, we need to be silent. To listen. To be comfortable with the silence.

To know that in the multitude of words—spoken/written only for the sake of speaking/writing—there is great potential for unwisely spoken/written words.

So silence, listening, and learning will come to the forefront today.

Today, I will be still and know.

This post first appeared on PetalsfromtheBasket.com on May 30, 2013.

WHY I SCHEDULE TIME WITH GOD

"The first day, God knows. The second day, you know. By the third day, everybody knows." I would cringe nearly every time my mom shared this with me—which was often—because I knew she was right. And few of us like to readily admit that "mama knows best!" Yet, the older we get, the more we realize that she actually did know best!

Neglecting to spend time in Bible study, prayer, heavenward meditation, or a combination of any or all of these doesn't go unnoticed. Now be careful, because it's not about placing a check mark on your "I'm a good Christian because I do these things" list. ("It" being "devotions," "personal Bible study," "God-and-I time," etc.) It's a choice to talk to and learn from the Creator of the universe, who willingly sent His only Son to die in my stead (because of my sin, present since birth, that causes me to fall short of God's glory) because of an unconditional love that never fails. (Can I get a hallelujah on that sentence alone? Wow!)

It's more like having the privilege to place a check mark on your list of "Because of all He's done, I want to do this ('this' being equivalent to the 'it' above) so that I can be a better Christian—be more like Christ!"

So I daily choose to place an allotted time on my calendar for "God-and-I Time" (GAIT). I call it that because I view it as an appointment I need to keep, a meeting I need to attend, and a commitment I need to honor. You are probably much better than I am about "just doing it," but I find that if I don't literally schedule it into my day, I neglect that time because I allow other things to so easily crowd their way into my schedule, usually because the evil ick tells me those things matter more (as if!).

How much time? That varies. I would encourage you not to set a specific time range—e.g., thirty minutes or sixty minutes. Just listen as you read, reply in prayer, and let each day's lesson guide you through and strengthen you for that day's journey. It's an appointment that's worth keeping!

This post first appeared on PetalsfromtheBasket.com on November 12, 2014.

THE NEED FOR CLEAN HEARTS
AND CLEAN CARPET

My precious friend Amy calls it carpet-smelling prayer. In Luke 5:12 (NASB), the Bible uses the idea of "falling on your face" before the Lord in prayer: "While He was in one of the cities, behold, there was a man covered with leprosy; and when he saw Jesus, he fell on his face and implored Him, saying, 'Lord, if You are willing, You can make me clean.'"

I think the motivation behind a prayer with this much emotion, this much passion, this much desire comes from the action described in the four words that precede his falling on his face before the Lord: "when he saw Jesus."

Oh sure, we read about Jesus. We talk about Jesus. Shoot, we even sing about Jesus. But when was the last time we *saw* Jesus?

No I'm not being mystical or speaking of physically viewing the living, breathing Son of God sitting across the room. I'm speaking of a much deeper view: a view that transcends mere vision.

For example, when I truly see Him for who He is and think of the Lord as my shepherd, I don't merely envision a male human being tending bleating sheep. I don't even simply picture the Lord Himself walking with me, staff in one hand, my hand in the other, as I find rest beside still waters—as awesome as that thought is. When I know Him and have a firsthand understanding of the depth of His character, I see in that title "shepherd" the overwhelming truth that because of who He is, "I shall not want." It encompasses the entirety of His being, His power, and His love.

Therein lies the problem. We fail to see—truly see—Jesus.

No, wait. I need to speak in the first person, teaching these truths to myself first. So let me rewrite that previous statement: *I* fail to see—truly see—Jesus.

So then here's the centuries-old question: Why do I continue in those things that distract me from seeing Jesus?

While there are many reasons for taking my eyes off of Jesus, perhaps the second chapter of the book of First John sums up the top three the best: "Do not love the world nor the things in the world. If anyone loves the world, the love of the Father is not in him. For all that is in the world, the lust of the flesh and the lust of the eyes and the boastful pride of life, is not from the Father, but is from the world" (verses 15–16, NASB).

It's that pesky "boastful pride of life" that seems to be effective at taking my eyes off of Jesus. But it might not be in the way that seems most obvious. The problem comes because I know my own sinfulness. When I use the eyes of truth to view who I am, I focus on those past sins and evil desires and—come on now, I know I can't be the only one—I think "He's not going to hear me anyhow because I just can't seem to 'get all the sin out!'" So I remain quiet.

Oh the pride in the delusion that my unworthiness is greater than His grace.

But there's that word: grace. The grace that He gives me over and over and over and over is given unconditionally, unceasingly, and undeservedly. It's the grace that makes Him God and leaves me in need of a God of grace.

And it is in remembering that grace that I let go of that to which I held so tightly, and in the letting go, my gaze turns to Jesus.

And in gazing upon Jesus, I am compelled to fall upon my face in the adoration that flows from "carpet-smelling prayer."

This post first appeared on PetalsfromtheBasket.com on October 27, 2014.

PERFECT STRENGTH

I stayed up late last night to write. I planned on catching up on this blog site as well as on my self-titled site (BrendaStrohbehn.com), where I "encourage and equip others to share their stories" and where I'm so far behind on my writing schedule that I'm often tempted to scratch the whole thing and start over.

That's a common trait of true perfectionism: if it can't be perfect, don't do it. (With a true perfectionist, this only applies to the areas that matter most to him or her. In other words, not everything has to be perfect.)

But I'm not a perfect person, so if I wait for perfection, nothing will ever get done.

So I went into analytical mode this morning and began to think about what keeps me from writing not only what I want to write but also what I should write.

Sometimes I just plain talk too much, and that makes my posts (and e-mails to friends) long and storytellerish. Sometimes I say too little, leaving readers uncertain of my meaning or feeling that I'm not concerned enough. Sometimes I want to be funny, and I'm not. Sometimes I don't mean to be funny, and I am. Sometimes I don't care enough about what others think. Sometimes I fear what others are going to think. Sometimes I even worry that I don't have the correct number of opposing "sometimes" pairings in my list!

But I think the important thing to do is to keep writing. Keep learning. Keeping making mistakes so that I can learn from them—even in areas unrelated to my writing.

Because when I do that, I see the power in the well-known Bible verse: "I can do all things through Him Who gives me strength" (Philippians 4:13, NIV). He tells us that He strengthens us because He knows that we need His strength! We can't possibly do it on our own because…get ready for it…we're not perfect.

But Christ is, making him the perfect Source of Strength!

So I'll give my best, do my best, expect my best, and never settle for less than the best, moving forward in the strength that He provides.

Now if you'll excuse me, I've got some writing to do.

_____

_____

_____

_____

_____

_____

_____

_____

_____

This post first appeared on PetalsfromtheBasket.com on September 5, 2014.

RAINY NIGHTS AND FAVORITE THINGS

My friend Shelley frequently creates a list as her Facebook post. She simply lists five things, varied in their scope, and concludes with these words: "These are a few of my favorite things." I actually look forward to reading her lists and find them encouraging; they also serve as great reminders to be grateful for the little things in life!

> "Be thankful in all circumstances, for this is God's will for you who belong to Christ Jesus." —I Thessalonians 5:18, NLT

It's raining tonight in my new little town in Northern Indiana, and after seeing Shelley's post today and listening to the rain, I was reminded of the scene in *The Sound of Music* when Maria, the governess, helps to alleviate the children's fear of the storm by singing the words, "These are a few of my favorite things." So, I decided that I could do a podcast and sing the song to post here, or I could stop and list even just a few of the many things for which I can be thankful tonight—and always. Lucky for you, I chose the latter!

> Neighbors that are so dear I can already share secrets with them. New friends who make an inconvenient effort to include me in their plans. Pretty journals in which to write plain thoughts, where I can create beauty from the ordinary. Text messages that include an

overabundance of exclamation points. Seeing my dad's eyes light up when my mom enters the room. Seeing my mom's eyes light up when my dad enters the room. The reignited desire for someone's eyes to light up when I enter the room. Having a day with no work assignments due and not having to panic about the hours with no specific income. Liquid chalk with which to create artistic daily calendars that help my parents differentiate between the long days and even longer nights. Opportunities to give as I have received. Bible verses on Post-it notes. Bubble baths that include candlelit quietness. Completed months with great memories. New months with fresh grace.

These are a few of my favorite things. What are some of yours?

This post first appeared on PetalsfromtheBasket.com on May 1, 2014.

THE DIFFERENCE BETWEEN POTENTIAL
& POSSIBILITIES

Before continuing my pre-Easter reading of the Book of John this morning, I was thinking of how—to my detriment, in most cases—I see potential in nearly everything and everyone. (I think it's a Pollyanna-related thing!)

Potential Involves My Plans

It hit me in an "aha-moment" kind of way that looking at potential is, for me, generally a way of envisioning how my plans would look if they were carried out—either in myself or in others. I thought about it far too long this morning and added "focusing only on potential" to my "part-of-me" elements that I need to lay on the altar before my God.

This very thing seemed to play out in the early verses of John chapter five: a man had been ill for thirty-eight years, and as he lay by the healing pool of Bethesda, he saw the potential that its water held. In fact, he even tried to avail himself of it to fulfill his own plan for healing but could never make it into the water on his own.

Christ's Power Includes Possibilities

But then Jesus came! When the man received the power of Christ's healing, he was not only healed of his illness but great possibilities were now before him. In fact, Scripture tells us elsewhere that "with God, all things are possible" (Matthew 19:26, NIV)!

Because he had the power of Christ, the potential of his plans turned into actual possibilities!

Lord, may I change my focus today from potential (in myself and others) that suits my plans to a focus on Your power and the possibilities that it offers!

This post first appeared on PetalsfromtheBasket.com on April 5, 2014.

LITTLE PINK CURLERS

When I think of Saturday nights, I think of little pink sponge rollers. You know the kind, right? The two-inch plastic curler is made up of a fold-over "frame." One half of it is a post over which the sponge tube fits; the other half, rectangular in shape so that it fits around the outside of the sponge tube. The frame clips shut at the top, holding the hair tightly in place.

For little girls, it's almost a rite of passage to get to wear these seemingly magic curlers to bed on Saturday night. At the age of five, nothing made me feel more like a princess (and probably look less like one—Ha-ha!) than having bouncy, ridiculously tight curls on Sunday morning! Sitting on the floor in front of mom on Saturday night and making sure to look straight ahead was more than a promise of "perky" hair. It was a way of preparing my mind that something special was going to happen the next day.

Now, forty-six years later, the role of the little pink curlers has been replaced by nail polish and lotions.

Nearly every Saturday night, I mentally place the activities of the past week into their proper "compartments" and take a little time to slow the pace a bit. The weekly manicure, consisting of filing, exfoliating, soaking, polishing, and moisturizing, serves to prepare my "grownup mind" that something special is going to happen the next day. (In fact, tonight's preparation will also include a pedicure for me. Tomorrow is "Barefoot Sunday" since we are being encouraged to donate our shoes before we leave so that they may be given to those who have no shoes!)

But it's not about the nails. Mine are simple and nothing you'll see on a magazine cover. It's about preparing body, soul, and spirit for what is to come.

Meeting with other believers for the sake of learning about and praising God with our worship deserves such intentional preparation—and more! So, with my newly painted nails and a relaxed body and soul, I will head to bed soon, prepared for a time of presleeping prayer, asking God to show Himself to me and to teach me what He longs for me to learn tomorrow at church.

Yes, schedules are busy. Not every Saturday night allows for leisurely pampering and restful activity. However, I encourage you to remember that one of the best ways to have a prepared heart in church on Sunday morning is to intentionally begin that preparation on Saturday night.

"Commit your works to the Lord, and your plans will be established." —Proverbs 16:3, NASB

This post first appeared on PetalsfromtheBasket.com on April 29, 2012.

LISTENING TO THE TOMATOES

I should have seen it coming when my mother named the tomato plants this year. When my parents' friend Jack brought my mother six plants for the patio, she got that look in her eye, and by the next morning, the two tomato plants that even the best farmer in the land would envy and the four pepper plants that are a deep shade of green yet to be named by Crayola had names: Kristi and Kylie are the tomatoes, and Karli, Kari, Kelli, and…oh, I can never remember the last one…are the pepper plants.

I think Jack must have somehow slipped my mother adoption papers when he delivered the first-rate produce, packed in just the right blend of soil, because we talk about these plants as if they were literal children: "I just gave Kristy a drink of water; she was looking pretty thirsty." "We need to see if the girls have grown any today." You know, normal talk like that!

But this morning the plants talked back. No, not literally—we're not that odd!

But as I sat on the patio to have my God-and-I-Time (the time each day when I read and meditate on portions of the Bible and spend some time in prayer, claiming that day's "new mercies" that I so desperately need), the plants were right in my line of vision, just a few feet away on the edge of the patio. I looked at the large "big beef" tomato that is turning an anticipatory shade of reddish orange and will be ready to pick in a day or two, and I listened with my heart to the lesson that God was using His "preaching plants" to teach me.

When my parents' friend dropped off the plants, they were already in great condition. Someone had nurtured them right from the start with the very best of the best, and it showed. They were thriving!

Then they were taken from their secure, comfortable surroundings and placed on our back porch. There they had to acclimate to the new conditions, and their caretakers (the silly ladies who call them by human names) had to adjust to caring for them in the best way possible, knowing: how much water to add, when to add the water, where to place the water (in the center of the plant, around the edges, or in the tray in which the pot is sitting), etc.

The well-being of the plants fluctuated for a few days, sometimes looking great and sometimes causing trepidation that we had ruined Jack's beautiful gifts to my parents.

Then, when they were doing well enough to earn accolades of "oohs" and "ahs" and numerous "likes" on Facebook photos of them (I told you: they're like family!), it seemed as if they were invincible.

Then it came. The massive storm front swept through our little town around 12:50 a.m., its entry announced via the loud-but-helpful-and-therefore-appreciated blaring of the town's tornado siren. The wind was fierce but thankfully not tornadic. The driving rains pelted the helpless plants in spite of their careful placement in the back corner of the patio when "Mike the Weatherman" had spoken of the impending storm.

The next morning, just after six hours with no power concluded, Mom and I headed out to the patio to "check on the girls." They looked beaten down—sad, almost. In fact, there were some losses. Two tomatoes well on their way to reaching maximum size and just before starting to change from the chameleon-like shade of green that matched the leaves to the subtle hints of oncoming red were lying on the cement, several feet from the branches that once provided nourishment and strength. The six plants each looked weak and weather-worn.

As the sun finally broke through and shone down on the patio and its inhabitants that day, the leaves began to reach out, seeming to know that their need for sustenance could only be fulfilled in doing so. It wasn't long before they were holding their heads high, as if rejuvenated for having survived so great a storm. The brutal winds that had beaten upon them and the strong rains that had nearly drowned their ability to survive were now being overcome by the determination to use those circumstances to increase—not relinquish—their strength.

So as I sat on the small wrought iron bench this morning, noticing that the plants, only one day later, looked stronger after the storm than before, the message they sent me was clear: trials might knock us down, cause us to feel like we're drowning in the struggle for mere survival, and make us doubt our ability to keep growing and moving forward, but those very trials are often the impetus for reaching outward for help and heavenward for guidance. And in doing so, we will once again thrive.

But it doesn't end there. Today for lunch my parents and I shared a giant—and I do mean giant—bright red "big beef" tomato (one that had been picked prior to the storm and had therefore weathered it well in the security of its placement on the kitchen counter during its final stages of ripening)! And for supper we had…what else but fried green tomatoes, truly serving as a reminder that even when things seem to be "lost," there is hope!

Oh, and in the spirit of Julie Andrews's line in the *Sound of Music* upon remembering the name of the young child whose name she had forgotten, "That's it—God bless Curt," I will conclude by stating that I just remembered the name of the last pepper plant: God bless Kodi.

"Each time he said, 'My grace is all you need. My power works best in weakness.' So now I am glad to boast about my weaknesses, so that the power of Christ can work through me." —2 Corinthians 12:9, NLT

This post first appeared on PetalsfromtheBasket.com on July 3, 2014.

TWO AWESOME TRUTHS

As with any major life change, the search for employment brings with it many highs and lows. I mentioned the other day the myriad of questions that seem to enter my mind uninvited, so I won't revisit their rude desire to inhabit my thoughts! Instead, I want to share two very simple but awesome thoughts that were shared with me today.

But first, I must stop to insert how greatly these truths served to remind me of the need for godly counsel. Not listening ears. Not someone with whom to "vent." Not just catchy phrases shared to make me "feel better." No. Today I was blessed with good, properly motivated, biblically based, godly counsel. And that is unbeatable—don't settle for less!

> "Your statutes also are my delight; they are my counselors."
> —Psalm 119:24, NASB

The first awesome thought, from a family member, was "revisit the truth."

Satan is the father of lies and is therefore the master "truth twister." It's easy to read God's Word and to know the Lord of all creation is in control, but I will transparently tell you that it's also easy to listen to the distorted truths presented to me by the evil one in the form of questions: "But why…?" "But how…?" "Why won't God tell me what's ahead—I need to know today, don't I?"

But if I stop in the middle of my thought to revisit the truth, I am reminded of *many* truths. Here are just a couple of those:

> "As for God, his way is perfect: The LORD's word is flawless; he shields all who take refuge in him."
> —II Samuel 22:31, NIV

> "So be strong and courageous! Do not be afraid and do not panic before them. For the Lord your God will personally go ahead of you. He will neither fail you nor abandon you."
> —Deuteronomy 31:6, NLT

The second thought, from a corporate employment specialist who is a believer and a friend, was just as awesome as the first! He reminded me that oftentimes in the process of making a job change it is easy to lose confidence (sound familiar?) and to lose hope. He said, "That's when your head droops, and you being looking down. But when you look down at your feet, that's the time to remember that you're on a solid foundation! So instead of losing hope, let that downward glance cause you to look up to One Who has it all under control!"

> "I look to you for help, O Sovereign Lord. You are my refuge…."
> —Psalm 141:8, NLT

There is actually a third awesome thought that I would like to add here, and that is this: these same awesome thoughts apply to all of us.

Whatever the need, whatever the sorrow, whatever the loss, whatever the questions that are coming into our minds, His truths are unchanging! So revisit the truth, and keep looking up to the Source of your solid foundation!

This post first appeared on PetalsfromtheBasket.com on April 17, 2012.

ABOUT THE AUTHOR

As the youngest of four children, Brenda has probably heard—and, according to her, fulfilled—every "spoiled youngest child" joke out there! She is an avid fan of Notre Dame football, and though she finds all flowers inspirationally beautiful, yellow roses and every color of hydrangea are her flowers of choice.

Another element that adds beauty to her days is music. Even though she no longer uses her degree in music education vocationally, she plays piano, flute, and mountain dulcimer, and she loves to sing!

Brenda loves to express herself through her writing and to help others do so as well. She coauthored a women's Bible study (with her mother, Lorraine), *But God*, and has completed writing and editing assignments for communications firms, businesses, websites, churches, schools, and colleges.

In addition to the proofreading, editing, and publishing preparation (PEP) she does through her freelance business, PEP Writing Services, Brenda is also an outsourced editor for a large POD (print on demand) company and proofreads for a communications firm that specializes in creating materials for the auto industry.

Brenda also maintains her faith-based blog, Petals from the Basket (found at PetalsfromtheBasket.com), and a blog and resource site for encouraging and equipping writers: BrendaStrohbehn.com.

She currently lives in Indiana, working from home and assisting her aging parents with their care.

18047506R00080

Made in the USA
San Bernardino, CA
29 December 2014